Feng Shui Living

 W9-BZX-876

Feng Shui Living

Sharon Stasney

Sterling Publishing Co., Inc. New York

A Sterling/Chapelle Book

Chapelle, Ltd.

- Jo Packham
- Sara Toliver
- Cindy Stoeckl

- Editor: Lana Hall
- Photography: Kevin Dilley for Hazen Photography
  Sharon Stasney
- Editorial Director: Caroll Shreeve
- Art Director: Karla Haberstich
- Copy Editor: Marilyn Goff
- Graphic Illustrator: Kim Taylor
- Staff: Burgundy Alleman, Kelly Ashkettle, Areta Bingham, Ray Cornia, Emily Frandsen, Susan Jorgensen, Barbara Milburn, Lecia Monsen, Suzy Skadburg, Desirée Wybrow

The copy, photographs, instructions, illustrations, and designs in this volume are intended for the personal use of the reader and may be reproduced for that purpose only. Any other use, especially commercial use, is forbidden under law without the written permission of the copyright holder.

Every effort has been made to ensure that all information in this book is accurate. However, due to differing conditions, tools, and individual skills, the publisher cannot be responsible for any injuries, losses, and/or other damages which may result from the use of the information in this book.

This volume is meant to stimulate decorating ideas. If readers are unfamiliar or not proficient in a skill necessary to attempt a project, we urge that they refer to an instructional book specifically addressing the required technique.

Library of Congress Cataloging-in-Publication Data

Stasney, Sharon.
  Feng Shui living / Sharon Stasney.
    p. cm.
  ISBN 1-4027-0347-3
  1. Feng shui. I. Title.
BF1779.F4S792 2003
133.3'337--dc21
                          2003008827
10 9 8 7 6 5 4 3

Published by Sterling Publishing Co., Inc.
387 Park Avenue South, New York, NY 10016
©2003 by Sharon Stasney
Distributed in Canada by Sterling Publishing
c/o Canadian Manda Group, 165 Dufferin Street
Toronto, Ontario, Canada M6K 3H6
Distributed in Great Britain by Chrysalis Books Group PLC
The Chrysalis Building, Bramley Road, London W10 6SP, England
Distributed in Australia by Capricorn Link (Australia) Pty. Ltd.
P.O. Box 704, Windsor, NSW 2756, Australia
Printed in China
All Rights Reserved

Sterling ISBN 1-4027-0347-3

Write Us

If you have any questions or comments, please contact:
  Chapelle Ltd., Inc.
  P.O. Box 9252, Ogden, UT 84409
  (801) 621-2777 • (801) 621-2788 Fax
  e-mail: chapelle@chapelleltd.com
  web site: chapelleltd.com

Introducing: the evocative home for feng shui living

Homes are like clothes. We all have our favorite clothes—the ones we wear hot out of the dryer. We don them, time and again, because they support living. In our favorites, we feel more comfortable, more spontaneous, more alive. The best homes are equally evocative. They coax us into living more, playing more, and interacting more with the world. Evocative homes work because they are full of "living spaces." Just as texture, softness, and form can turn an ordinary white T-shirt into a favorite, the colors, materials, and structures of a home can leave us feeling extraordinary.

The focus of this book is how our homes can make us feel more alive. They accomplish this because they provide both safety and "stretch." Good homes support the individuals who live in them and honor who they are, yet those same homes challenge their owners, encouraging them to take one more step toward whom they want to become. They interweave past, present, and future, anchoring us in tradition while "opening" us in possibility.

Home needs to be a place to practice the art of living that feels safe and supportive. Like a good therapist, a home can baby-step us into greater awareness and acknowledgment of our gifts and tendencies, and create the space in which to practice. In the safety of our homes, we try out our many-faceted selves to decide which of those facets we want to bring out for public viewing.

Evocative homes can coax us into living more, playing more, and interacting more with the world.

Are these experiences only for the rich, who are able to design their homes from the ground up? Luckily, evocative homes do not require a budget; rather they require attention to two primary patterns: safety and expansion. You can create an evocative home by asking and answering for yourself the following two questions:

How can I create safety in my home?

How can I use my home to embrace life more fully?

Through focusing on how your home creates safety and expansion, you can turn any structure, no matter how small, strange, or seemingly insignificant, into a beautiful and powerful "living space."

Table of Contents

The turtle's shell has been a feng shui symbol of safety for many centuries.

This sandstone armchair is the perfect feng shui seat. With a high supportive back, low supportive sides, and an open expanse in front, this chair would make anyone sitting in it feel safe and in control.

Places of safety

Feng shui priority number one is safety. You must feel safe and comfortable before you can risk expansion and growth. This means the most important overriding feng shui principle is creating safety in your home. You have probably read quite a few feng shui tips that related to safety, but never pulled all of them together into one category before. For example, Form School feng shui, the mother of all feng shui approaches, teaches that you should have the turtle at your back and the phoenix in front of you. In rather cryptic terms, what this is saying is to support your back (as a turtle in its shell) and provide open expansive energy in front (the phoenix represents transformation and expansion). Only when the back is supported can the front, the more public part of you, expand. To expose your back, such as placing your home on a cliff edge, weakens you. It drains chi and makes feeling safe difficult to achieve.

The mirrored wall in this living room gives everyone a view of comings and goings. It equalizes what would otherwise be a striking inequality in the safety of various "sit" spots.

A commanding view

If you have ever been blindfolded and led around by the hand, you know just how scary it is to not know what is in front of you or coming up behind you. Being able to see who or what is coming is comforting because it gives you a moment to decide how you want to respond.

If you are sitting so that you cannot see the door, turn your seat around, if possible. It is best to place as much of your energy in front of you as possible. If your desk is attached to the wall, or some other feature prevents you from turning to face your door, place a convex mirror to open up your view while seated.

 This chair is the least desirable place to sit, as the mirror exposes the back of this seat to everyone.

When your back is protected, as with the wall or screen, you feel safer.

The mirrored wall shown here allows anyone seated to see the door into the room, increasing a feeling of safety. If you are sitting so that you cannot see the door, turn your seat accordingly.

Solid wall behind you

No sitting area feels safe that has an exposed back. Just like the turtle in his shell, human beings feel better when have they some sort of protection behind them. Although a solid wall is the best form of protection, a sofa table or plant behind a sitting area is better than nothing there at all. Additionally, partial walls can be constructed through the creative use of screens, hanging fabric panels, or beaded curtains.

The right armchair (above) has an exposed back, which makes it feel unsafe. By turning the chair just a bit (below), it feels safer because the chair has more of its back against the wall.

Include retreat spaces

No one feels brave and courageous every day. If home holds places where you can retreat when feeling vulnerable or when you need a little time to regroup, it reduces your stress and anxiety levels. Set up to comfort the physical body and restore the spirit; retreat spaces have ways of filtering out the influence of the outside world. Such a filter could be a great sound system that floods the room with uplifting music. Another filter might be a protected view of passersby, so that you can watch but not be seen. One of my favorite filters is unplugging the phone and sitting down by the fire for an evening of board games with my two boys. If your home holds places where you can escape when things get to be too much, you will risk more, try harder, and push life to its envelope. When there is no place to retreat to, you will always hold part of yourself back.

This cozy window seat is tucked into a kitchen corner, making it possible to be close to other family members and still retreat. Any retreat space with a window is a great way to maintain connection with the outside world while rejuvenating your spirit.

Eliminate potential dangers

Remember the last time you had a horrible deadline hanging over you, invading your sleep and filling you with dread. Placing shelves with items on them directly above where someone will be sitting is the physical counterpart to that undesirable state. A common place to find such shelves is in the bathroom directly above the toilet. To exacerbate the sense of impending doom, the shelf is usually shallow and the items hang over the edge. If you have existing shelves that you cannot move, fill them with lightweight objects such as baskets, towels, or a stack of pillows. Heavy or breakable items like books, pottery, vases, or glass knickknacks should be avoided.

This country room commits a number of feng shui sins. For starters, the propped picture above the fireplace has breakable items stacked in front of it. The potential that the picture could slip down, knocking all the breakables to the floor, creates constant unrest in the room. Other sins include breakable items on the floor, such as this vase, and a blocked fireplace.

Dirt is your friend. Just bringing in a potted plant will increase Earth energy in your home. Consider an indoor atrium, a miniature garden in a pot, or herbs growing in the kitchen. Plants link you to nature's cycles, as well as her grounding, reminding you that chi cycles through phases. Tuning in to nature's cycles can help you bring your life into balance and your home into harmony with the environments with which it is inextricably meshed.

Potted plants are powerful yet simple ways to bring Earth inside to ground spirit.

He who plants a garden, plants happiness.

—Chinese proverb

Bring nature inside by using unadorned windows to open the garden view. Outdoor elements such as live plants and patio furniture can also be used indoors to increase Earth energy.

Connect to nature's grounding

Nothing helps you feel safer than connecting your own energy to something as large and stable and nurturing as Mother Earth. The physical earth can hold all of your stress and anxiety, and replace those feelings with a calm serenity that is hard to find elsewhere. When you learn to bring your body into connection with the earth's energy field, this is called grounding. You naturally feel steady, calm, and able to let go of any excess energy. The best way to ground your home is to bring Mother Earth inside. If you have ever spent time in a third-world country, walking on dirt floors and surrounded by straw walls, you have felt the powerful presence of Earth in the home. You can bring this presence into more-modern homes by contrasting polished surfaces with rough primitive textures, replacing plastics and synthetics with organic materials, and complementing overhead lighting with the warm glow of lit candles.

Containers

Containers are everywhere, in collections of antique glassware, coffee tins, carved wooden bowls, and woven baskets. Containers gather chi, helping you feel that there will be enough when you need it. They enclose and hold you and your things, uniting your need for psychological support with your material possessions. They represent Earth energy; and, just as soil that cannot hold rain cannot sustain life, a home without adequate containers cannot hold chi. In such a place, you will not feel supported or safe.

Full containers. If all your containers are full, your Earth energy tends toward the smothering and possessive side. Since full containers are a grounding energy, one that holds a pattern in place, too many full containers make it difficult to move your chi and do not allow for change. Disease and emotional difficulties can come as much from sluggish chi as from chi that moves too quickly. Break through excessive Earth with Wood energy. Place something green or tall in each container that must remain full, and remove as many unnecessary containers as possible. The traditional feng shui adjustment is to place bamboo (live or dried) in the container. Bamboo is considered the most aggressive wood element, breaking up even the hardest earth.

Empty containers. If you have a lot of empty containers, this is a strong indicator that you look to external sources for happiness and demand that others meet your needs because you feel unable to fill those needs yourself. Empty containers, in general, symbolize your inactivated potential. Although the pot has the ability to hold chi, it currently holds nothing. Sprinkling a few grains of rice in each container is a strong feng shui cure. The grains represent your ability to activate your potential and connect directly to the source (rice represents universal chi) rather than another person.

The ultimate in containerizing, this built-in Shaker wall unit is as beautiful as it is functional. You will want to put your things away if you create a beautiful and organized place to put them. A few hours spent with a professional organizer and a trip to the container store can change how you relate to "stuff" in general. Take the time to start enjoying all those things you worked so hard to acquire.

Make your containers suit your style. This ladder rack is more than a display item for vintage baskets, it provides useful storage and a playful approach to containerizing. If, like this owner, you do not want to fill all those baskets, be certain you put a couple of grains of rice in each one to keep the space energized.

Written intentions placed in a locked box or a letter hidden behind a mirror on the wall are ancient feng shui rituals for holding energy patterns in place.

If you have a home that holds no secret spaces, no hidden hole behind a sliding panel, no cubby underneath loose floorboards, make your own secret place. Hide it from company's eyes and limit access to it, such as this locked desk in the corner of a room accomplishes.

We always fold ourselves away from others just enough to preserve a secret or two, something that we cannot share without destroying our inner landscape.
—Anne Roiphe

Secret spaces

We all have parts of us that have been lost, concealed from ourselves as well as from the outside world. Secret places are where we can rediscover that which has been lost. Once discovered, the hidden parts of ourselves can remain private until we feel ready and able to bring them out, piece by piece, into the world. In his book, *The Poetics of Space*, Gaston Bachelard expresses this fundamental human need:

"Wardrobes with their shelves, desks with their drawers, and chests with their false bottoms are veritable organs of the secret psychological life. Indeed, without these 'objects' and a few others in equally high favor, our intimate life would lack a model of intimacy. . . . It is not merely a matter of keeping a possession well guarded. The lock doesn't exist that could resist absolute violence, and all locks are an invitation to thieves. The lock is a psychological threshold. . . ."

You have a right to keep secrets. Secrecy provides the safety to be intimate and rigorously honest. Intimacy and honesty are absolutely necessary in getting to know and embrace yourself completely.

Closets can become intimate altars, secret spaces, and personal havens.

Closets

Closets are a form of secret space. They have always been associated with the "shadow" aspects of the personality, a place to hide those things that the public persona does not wish to acknowledge or expose. "Coming out of the closet" and "skeletons in the closet" are two English phrases that reveal this association. More than just a place to hide or keep things secret, however, closets are also a place to put things on hold, allowing something to lie dormant and unexercised for a while. No one has the energy to deal with everything all at once. You need to be able to put some things aside to focus your energy. A home without closets feels unbearably exposed and overwhelming, and a psyche without enough quiet places to store things is equally so.

Closets as secret spaces. I remember sitting in my mother's closet, trying on her shoes, coats, shawls, and hats. It was a way of "trying out" different possible futures, seeing myself as a grownup before I had to take on all the responsibilities of one.

Your closets be as havens. They can keep things confidential and safe until you are ready to expose them. They can allow you a trial run with minimal risk. They can support your hidden desires through the pictures you paste up behind the wall of clothes hanging in your wardrobe.

Do not limit the function of your closets to storage. They can house intimate altars, function as meditation rooms, or become adventure caves for your children. Whatever you want to keep secret from the world, you can place in a closet. Closets will give you the time and space you need to figure out how to express that part of you in a graceful, balanced way.

Full closets. You might think that full closets are the result of not having enough closets, but that is not the full feng shui meaning. Full closets indicate that the cycle of accumulation (a yin phase) is out of balance with the cycle of dispersion (a yang phase). Regardless of how many closets you have, the goal is balance. That means spending as much time and energy dispersing the items you no longer need as you do accumulating new items.

Regardless of how much closet space you have, you need to let go of as many objects as are necessary to live in your current space with "comfort" and "ease." Comfort means having the ability to care for your present-time need—letting go of what you might need in the future, as well as what you picked up in the past. Ease means you are able to access what you need in your closets quickly and efficiently, without digging through piles or pulling out layers of stuff to reach something at the very back.

Simply by organizing what is in your closet you can open up space.

I promise that the following process will bring order and success to your closet-clearing efforts:

- Think of your closets as a metaphor for your lungs. Chi needs to move in and out of the closet, just as air passes through your lungs. To get yourself ready to clear out your closet, open the door and leave it open for 24 hours prior to the clearing.
- Pull everything out and clean the floor. (All the heavy, lower-level vibrations sink to the floor over a period of time.)
- Sort your items into like piles, labeling each pile with a self-adhesive note as you create it.
- Place the least-used items back in the closet first, putting them toward the back and up high, where it is difficult to reach them.
- For closets that are stacked from top to bottom, use baskets or metal mesh containers to group the objects and to get them off the floor.
- For very full closets, consider painting the inside of the closet a bright yang color (a buttery yellow or a spring apple green) that will keep the chi moving even with all that stuff.
- Place the objects you use most in the front center portion of the closet, creating easy access.
- Step inside the closet and shut the door. If you have a hard time breathing, you need to let go of more.
- Continue releasing and reorganizing until you can go inside and breathe with ease—with the door shut.

16

Overexposing yourself

It is healthy to take risks, to open yourself to others, and to extend the hand of friendship. However, over-exposing yourself is more an indication of a desperate need for connection and intimacy than an inclination to be neighborly. Common forms of overexposure include leaving the front door open all the time, not covering windows so that people can see in (especially at night), leaving windows open so that neighbors can overhear private conversations, and going outside in clothing (underwear, revealing pajamas) that is inappropriate for social situations.

If you find you tend to expose yourself too much, look for ways that you can share and connect with others that bring balance and self-respect. You will know you are not sharing yourself in a balanced way when others do not give of themselves to you the way you give to them. This is not a matter of you being more gracious or openhearted than they are; it usually means your need for connection overwhelms your interactions with others to the point where they begin to push you away.

Before placing the screen, this kitchen is exposed to everyone in the living room.

Placing the screen allows the owner control over how much of her kitchen is seen.

Feng shui adjustments, such as this screen, are as beautiful as they are practical.

Paper piles. Too many items on the ground can work against you. However, if the environment is too heavy, or if you suffer depression or fatigue, you are experiencing too much of a good thing. One of the ways to lift the chi is to bring the items up off the floor just a few inches, so that energy can pass underneath. Place large heavy plants on plant stands that sit about three inches off the floor, stack items on shelves, replace the feet on couches or other furniture pieces, or even take a few items off the floor itself and place them on a table or shelf. Make these changes slowly, watching to be certain you are able to sustain your grounding without turning to other channels such as clutter, paper piles, or weight gain.

This entry hall benefited greatly from the addition of the few colorful pots of flowers, and a container for walking sticks. This is an example of how using objects on the floor to ground a room can be healthy. The white walls, hardwood floors, and intense color choices are strong yang components. They need something on the ground to pull the energy back down and help the space feel comfortable.

Items on the ground

Numerous items on the floor are often an attempt to "ground." Numerous factors in modern society will leave you seeking some grounding. Strong electromagnetic fields, virtual realities, an increasingly fast pace, and a lifestyle disconnected from nature's patterns and rhythms are only a few of these factors. As noted earlier in this chapter, grounding is the ability to forge a connection with the density and receptivity of Earth energy. An individual "grounds" in order to stabilize himself by connecting to the earth's enormous mass. Without enough grounding, you can feel scattered, distracted, full of inner turmoil, and confused.

If you find yourself placing numerous items low to the ground, ask yourself if you are trying to ground your energy. Items low to the ground will naturally bring your energy down lower in the body. When your energy settles into your *"dan tien,"* the body's natural energy center about four inches below the navel, you feel more grounded and connected to the natural world.

Furniture

The size, shape, and design of your furniture affects how comfortable you feel sharing your ideas and creations with others. To feel safe enough to share, your furniture needs to both support and express you.

A simple item with an unusual shape can express volumes.

Balanced furniture does not mean every piece must be the same size. Here, the large upholstered chair and substantial spool table are balanced by the shallow narrow book cabinet along the wall and the small chair that serves as a table or a footstool.

As tempting as it was to squeeze this tall armoire into the room, it actually constricts the chi flow because it does not leave enough space on top.

Streamlining your storage with built-ins eliminates the chi constriction and allows for more flow.

Larger-than-life furniture. When furniture is larger than the body that fills it, it feels much like a knight's armor, shielding you from the energy and opinions of others who might enter your space. Sometimes oversized furniture is necessary to fill an oversized room (See When your gathering place is too large on page 66), but it will make interactions more formal and limit how much people relax while in your home.

Find out what specific meaning your large furniture has for you by answering the question, "What kind of a person has large furniture?" Some responses I have heard to this question are:

- rich people,
- stately people,
- important people,
- fearful people,
- impostors,
- cold people.

Feng shui suggests that the size of a desk or a chair sends a strong message about how important you think you are. The ideal chair is one that supports your entire frame, comes high up the back, and provides armrests. If it is too large, however, it will dwarf you and make you look small and helpless inside it. The same goes for your desk, dining table, or living-room sofa. If you find that your furniture is too large, the following ways can help you soften its effects in your space.

- Add lamplight and dimmers to blur the harsh edges and straight lines of large furniture with soft light.
- Include a dynamic, organic focal point. A fish tank with lively colorful fish, an indoor atrium, or even a decorative bowl of wheat grass can draw the eye away from the furniture and make the space feel more lively.
- Drape slipcovers over dining chairs.
- Bring in smaller decor pieces that are playful in nature, such as a hand-painted lamp, a collage, or a humorous sculpture.

Walls

The purpose of a wall is to serve as a barrier from external forces and to provide support for the entire structure—the thick adobe of the southwest, the primitive concrete of a city loft, the whitewashed timbers of a California beach house.

Thick walls. Usually made from mud, brick, or plaster, thick walls are a wonderful way to provide supportive Earth energy. Thick Earth walls also allow for texture and aging, which connotes that support is long lasting, not temporary. If your walls are paper thin, they cannot physically support the weight of the house (See Cracked walls below) and do not help you feel safe or protected. Visually increase the thickness of your walls by texturizing existing walls (works over lathe and plaster and over Sheetrock®), adding a stucco finish, using a layered-paint technique, or wallpapering. These thickening techniques will also "age" your walls, increasing timeless feel.

Cracked walls. Cracked walls represent a damaged support system and need to be mended as soon as possible. Simply covering up or hiding cracked walls is not sufficient. Covering cracks simply means that you are ignoring the fact that you do not feel supported. If you continue to exert your energy to reach your objectives, without taking the time to reestablish your connections with external sources of support, you will wipe yourself out. When repairing cracked walls, put forth your best effort to repair strained or damaged relationships, reconnect with nature, or tune in to your inner connection to "Source."

Thick walls represent a strong support system and help people feel safe and supported by their environment.

Adding a textured finish thickens walls and increases the safety factor of the home.

Why not go out on a limb? That is where the fruit is.
—Will Rogers

The inspiring home

Stretch, grow, risk, challenge, deepen, expand, refine. Anchored in a safe, steady home, you are able to open and look at parts of yourself that would otherwise remain behind locked doors. However, a safe haven is only healing if you leave it once in a while. Safe colors, textures, and arrangements are meant to be the fodder for growth, not the ends in themselves. This is why a house with nothing but square shapes and brown earthy colors feels like it is missing something. Like the soil, the safe home, without elements of surprise, growth, and change, feels barren.

This lovely collection of South American art and colorful tapestries punctuate this sitting area with personality and style. It is the personal, the unexpected, and the bold that give a room its zip.

Let yourself soar

Safety features anchor chi in the home, moving it low to the ground and slowing the flow. Chi that has slowed to a standstill brings stagnation, fatigue, and disease. Homes must also contain features of expansion to balance this slowing. The symbol for expansion in Form School feng shui is the phoenix. Just as the turtle protects its back, the phoenix rises up from the ashes, having transformed challenge and risk into soaring, unrestrained energy. The rising phoenix is not meant to stay chained to the earth; it heads for the open sky. Give your interior world sky, as well as earth, and your wings will unfold.

How does the philosophical concept of "sky" translate into interior design? All features that open your energy body, activate a stronger chi flow, and speed up the rate at which your chi is moving are expansion features. Chi needs to move up and out, pushing through any boundaries or blocks, to send your spirit soaring. A spot of blue in an otherwise brown vase, a silk scarf in a pile of linens, or a star-shaped pillow against a rectangular sofa, all surprise the eye and wake the sleepy chi.

Unexpected views; personalized collections; and unique combinations of colors, shapes, and structural elements are the interior alchemist's formula for a blue sky. Here a window frame in a garden bed adds a startling visual accent to excite the chi.

Disguise blank walls. Protective supporting walls are great, but not when they block your ability to expand. For example, walking through your front door to be greeted by a blank wall just a few feet in front of you is considered bad feng shui. Why? Because it cripples your ability to expand your chi immediately upon entering your home. The phoenix does not have enough time to get off the ground before its flight is stopped. If the eye can perceive something in the distance, the energy to move forward is mobilized. With no views into interior rooms, no enticing curve of color or form, those energy reserves are never activated.

A collection of miniature African masks brings interest to a previously blank wall.

Signs of growth

Plants that have outgrown their pots are not encouraged by the surrounding soil to continue growing. Likewise, home owners that have filled every last surface or bit of closet space are bound to feel stuck and stymied if they try to move forward. Of course, it is easier to repot your plants than it is to buy a new home every time you outgrow your existing one. Still, you have only three options. You can increase the size of your home by adding new rooms or closets, you can decrease the amount of things in the home, or you can organize those things in such a way as to open up more space between items. You need to decide which of these three options, or a combination of the three, is viable for you.

Increasing your space. Use the following ideas to rethink your storage space.

- An unused back porch can become a mud room with built-in storage cabinets.
- A decorative piece of furniture can be exchanged for an armoire that functions as a four-by-seven-foot closet.
- A staircase could be opened underneath to store seasonal objects.
- A new master suite could be reconfigured from an existing attic.

Give yourself the gift of open space!

An otherwise wasted wall area flanking a window became home to a pair of matching bookshelves with storage underneath, increasing the functionality as well as the beauty of the space.

Selecting gatekeepers

Clutter clearing is a hot feng shui topic; however, it is important to distinguish between "clutter clearing" and letting things go. For someone who stores precious objects or family heirlooms for future generations to think of these objects as clutter is next to impossible. These items are not junk, rather they are collected life experiences stored in material form. What, to an outsider, might look like a lot of knickknacks are life vignettes built over generations of use. For many, releasing the experiences from the forms is incredibly difficult—the two seem inseparable.

I use a process of transferral to help clients through this difficult stage. I ask them to select those objects that have the most luminosity surrounding them, that function as gatekeepers to entire chunks of family history. A client might be storing three different sets of china, for example, or many boxes of old clothes. Selecting these objects can be a time-consuming process and it is important to support the person during this time. Once a client selects these objects, the energy of other like objects can be transferred to the holding objects.

The transfer happens by placing a holding object next to a similar object and visualizing the light in the similar one moving over and increasing the luminosity of the holding object. Sometimes it helps clients to hold both items, so that they can feel this energy transfer take place. Once the life force of an object is transferred to the holding object, letting that item pass to another home is much easier.

Rearranging what is there. When common objects are grouped together, they require less space and less energy. A closet jam-packed with old clothes, sheets, journals, towels, and piles of board games can transform into an organized and functioning space by taking the time to sort, fold, tidy, and stack these items neatly.

The most wonderful part about getting organized is that when you place like items with like, they energetically meld into one item. Instead of carrying the emotional and energetic weight of dozens of separate items in any given closet, you meld these items into groupings of three or four. The time and energy it takes from you to manage these items in the future is greatly reduced.

Items such as these Buddhas, can function as gatekeepers, holding and storing the energy of an entire chunk of family history.

25

The risers and railings in a staircase lift eye, chi energy, and spirit.

Vertical lift

As your eye ascends, so does your chi. Pillars, columns, crown molding, and vertical structural features send chi energy spiraling upward. An interesting piece of wood at the top of a doorway, or the transfer of an outdoor porch pillar to your living room are unique expressions of vertical energy that can inspire your imagination as well as lift your chi. Imagination is the parent of creative expression, and light, high vibrations are most conducive to this mental art form. Look down at your feet and see how difficult it is to think creatively while gazing directly downward.

The carved wooden lintel brings the eye up above the doorway, raising the chi in the room.

Add a color splash

A startling burst of color can be just the thing to liven a drab room. Consider seasonal flowers, a throw, or candles as simple methods of including intense color without the overwhelm.

Find your edge

Although I am not an advocate of perching items precariously on shelves or other like surfaces, sometimes moving an item just an inch or two toward the edge of a table or mantel can completely change how "daring" the room feels.

A splash of color can increase your willingness to take risks.

This little horse perched just close enough to the edge of the mantel makes things interesting. Sometimes a single item is all that is needed to bring a sense of adventure into a room.

28

A few things I always ask my students about their pictures are:

- If you drew just the face of your house, do you rely on external sources to help you define who you are?
- If you drew people, do you see your home as relating to the people who live there?
- If you drew trees, plants, or other natural elements, do you feel connected to the natural world and able to draw comfort and strength from it?
- Is there any part of your house that exists, which you have failed to draw?
- If so, do you energetically cut yourself off from that part of the house?
- Is the house in your drawing accessible or hidden and isolated?

The right amount of exposure

As comfortable as it is to sit safely ensconced in your home, you need to venture out and connect with the outside world. One of my favorite workshop exercises is to have participants draw their homes on pieces of paper without giving them any guidelines or indications of what I will be looking for when they are done. (If you want to try this yourself, stop reading now and draw your house. Then continue reading to see what your drawing reveals about how you connect to the world.) Some draw their floor plan, others draw just the fronts of their houses, and others draw the inside, the outside, the city lights, the neighboring trees, the park around the corner, and the grocery store down the street.

What a person draws is a powerful indicator of how connected they feel to the world around them. If someone includes their pet cat but not their husband in their drawing, it may have interesting psychological implications. For those who link their house to the city by drawing streets but do not add a single tree, the implications are different, but nonetheless, richly revealing.

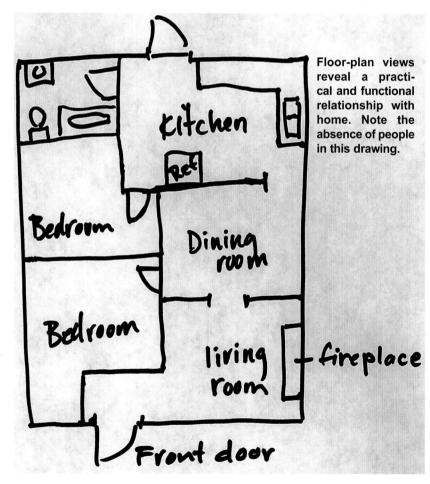

Floor-plan views reveal a practical and functional relationship with home. Note the absence of people in this drawing.

The originator of this drawing has connected her house to the natural world by including a tree, sun, grass, and surrounding shrubs.

This drawing indicates that the owner feels connected to the other people in the neighborhood. Roads (a means of access) have also been included.

This is the only drawing that includes people and pets in the home. Although it is a floor-plan drawing, the originator has used color and has also included live plants, revealing a connection to nature.

ME = MARCIE
TOM = HUSBAND
STACY = DAUGHTER
MARK = SON

Empty closets

In the last chapter, we talked about closets as secret spaces that empower you to try new things. Empty closets (and empty rooms) are a bit different. An empty closet indicates that the anabolic (breaking down) processes in a person's life are stronger than the catabolic (building up) processes. In the terms of Chinese medicine, the yang overwhelms the yin, creating an inability to hold onto much of anything for long, including friends, jobs, and hobbies. Empty closets also tend to reflect a life that is still on hold, waiting to be activated. Until there is purpose, there is no need to draw to you the things you need to fulfill that purpose.

To fill the empty closet, you need to connect to your life's purpose. In feng shui, purpose relates to "*li.*" Li is the natural, organic purpose as evident in form. As the veins in a leaf or the markings on jade, each organism has a natural pattern or expression that arises from within. Discovering and expressing your li is how you find your way in the natural flow and order of life. To find your li, place an item in the closet that displays its pattern, such as a shell or a rock. Leave the item in the closet for as long as it takes to attract to you the things you need to fulfill your purpose. Let it serve as a magnet, drawing the people, situations, opportunities, and resources you need to discover and give your gifts in the world.

If you are struggling to find a deeper sense of purpose, place a leaf in your empty closet. The leaf contains everything it needs within itself, its pattern artfully displayed as tiny veins across a papery membrane.

As the veins in a leaf or the markings on jade, each organism has a natural pattern or expression that arises from within.

This woven box can be used to catch, hold, and transform negative thoughts, fears, or emotions. As you interact with an empty room, identify and write down any fears or difficult emotions that come up for you and stuff them in your basket or container. The container will do the work of transforming them.

Rooms cut off from the rest of the house

Whether access to a room is physically limited or it just feels that way, some rooms are separate from the chi flow of the house. These rooms are dormant, rarely entered, and have a lower chi force. In some cases, usually when someone has lost their partner and is living alone in the house, an entire side of the house feels separate and lifeless.

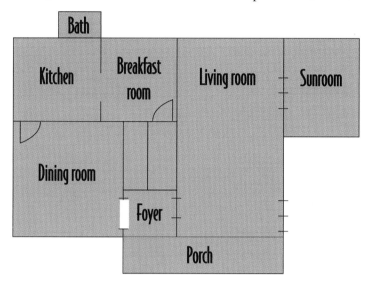

This house plan demanded that a door be opened from the foyer to the dining room, thus connecting it to the rest of the house. Before reconstruction, one had to walk from the foyer through the living room, the hallway, the breakfast room, and the kitchen to reach the dining room.

Ba gua map

Abundance	Fame/ reputation	Intimate relations
Family/ ancestors	Health	Children/ creativity
Self knowledge	Journey/ career	Helpful people

Entrance

Merging the room with the house. When one room is removed from the chi flow of the house, first figure out which ba gua sector the room is in. (See Ba gua map on page 110 also for more information on ba gua mapping.) Ask yourself how you are currently feeling about that area of your life. In what ways might you feel cut off or estranged? For example, if the room falls into Family and Ancestors, do you feel isolated or removed from your family circle in some way? Did you choose to leave for some reason? If the room falls into Helpful People, do you desire to be an accepted integral part of a thriving community, yet find yourself playing the role of the loner or outsider? If the room is in Self-knowledge, are you a stranger to your own inner needs and desires, afraid of spending time alone?

When you discover what part of your inner terrain is represented by your vacant or separate room, you will know whether you are ready and willing to reconnect with that part of you. If you are willing, you can begin the merger.

You will need one of three objects: a woven basket with a lid, a hollowed-out gourd, or a piece of pottery with a narrow neck at the top. These containers are traditionally used to catch, hold, and transform any negative thoughts, fears, or emotions. Place this object in the room. Next, unblock any doors or windows that do not open. If there is a door you can open but always leave shut, open the door. Draw back shades and blinds to allow as much "light of day" into the room as possible. Place something in the room that you will need to care for, such as a few plants, a fountain, or a pet bird.

Turn your face to the sunshine and all shadows fall behind.
—Helen Keller

The force of light

More than any other force, light represents nature's ability to bring life force into the home. A home that does not receive enough natural light gradually loses its life force and becomes unable to activate or energize the people living there. (See Illumination on pages 93–94 for information on how seasonal lighting affects the body.)

Sitting areas with access to a natural light draw comfort.

Natural light infuses this room with a vibrant intensity that lifts the spirit and energizes the body.

Light on two sides. Years ago, the authors of *A Pattern Language,* Alexander/Jacobson/Silverstein, made the claim that every room needs natural light on two sides in order to feel balanced. Without light on at least two sides of a room, the lit wall would be too bright, and the remaining space would fall into shadow. I have tested their statement for the past eight years and must agree that every room feels better if it has at least two walls that allow natural light into the room. This light does not need to come directly from a window, however. It is possible to get your light through a doorway into an adjacent room or by replacing part of an interior wall with glass block, an interior window, or a mirror.

A light in the tunnel. Some rooms are positioned directly in the center of the house and have no access to natural light at all. Solar tubes are a great modern invention that can solve this problem some of the time. Installed on the roof, a solar tube can bring light down a tube into rooms that have no exterior walls, such as an interior bathroom. However, if you have living space above you, you cannot use this method. Compensate for a lack of light by adding a fan and live green plants to the room. Clear out heavy items if you can and paint the walls a light color. These adjustments will increase the yang energy in the space and help balance the lack of light.

Adding windows on the right created a balanced flow of light and chi, making this room a delightful place to be. A similar effect could be achieved with a mirror.

This chair is too large for the room and creates a chi block.

Selecting a smaller chair for beside the fireplace brought the room back into balance.

Furniture

In the previous chapter, we addressed the issue of furniture that was too large. But furniture is much more than a place to sit. Your tables, chairs, lamps, and sofas are powerful vehicles for self-expression. A blue buffet in the dining room, a whimsical lamp shade, or an antique mail cupboard becomes a vessel by which the soul travels through the physical realm. These items are much more than decorative. Their painted surfaces reflect your smiles and the contents of their drawers reveal your dreams.

Diminutive furniture. When your furniture is too small, it is challenging to assert yourself. Your home base is communicating to you that you are small and insignificant. When guests come and sit in chairs that are too small to hold them, they will wonder if you are capable of taking care of yourself. Although smaller furniture is sometimes necessary in small spaces, make certain that you supplement small furniture pieces with an underlying message of strength and self-reliance.

- Add bold wall color or intense spots of color in your decor items.
- Use materials that last a long time, such as a leather couch or a hardwood desk.
- "Self-soothe" and care for your needs with candles, a stereo, and a comfy footstool.
- Add living plants to expand the chi and help your guests feel expansive, even if the chair they are sitting in is small.
- Place your wall art a few inches lower than normal to decrease the scale of the room and help the furniture feel larger.
- Add enough furniture so that the space does not have gaping holes where the chi flow stalls.

Simply opening a window can jump-start your chi and increase the energy in a room.

Too much furniture. The accumulation of stuff is the same for furniture as it is for other items. Too much slows the chi flow and prohibits movement, change, and the ability to take action. The more yin a person is, the greater the tendency to fill up every last inch of space. Start by getting the chi moving before you even move any furniture.

- Hang a large 40mm or 50mm round faceted crystal in the center of the room or home. The crystal will send chi out in 360 degrees, breaking up old and rigid patterns, making it easier for you to begin a new pattern.
- Open your windows and drapes more, letting in both light and fresh air.
- Turn your lights on more often, even during the day.

The furniture density in this room inhibits chi flow. To get the chi flowing here again, remove the trunks and replace them with a small side table. Straightening the ottoman and shifting the dining area a foot to the right would also improve the area.

When you are ready to remove furniture:

- Start by removing small pieces, such as an occasional table or an extra lamp.
- Remove pieces that block you from accessing other parts of the house—a chair that blocks a door, a dresser that keeps you from opening a window.
- Work slowly, one or two items at a time, allowing your body time to adjust to each change before you remove additional items.
- Find great new homes for the items you remove to create a win/win situation for all.
- Consider moving some favorite items to a porch, patio, or garden setting.

A wall of windows becomes its own canvas, allowing the owners of this room to view a constantly evolving display of color.

Walls

What is on the walls? Walls are the canvas, you are the artist. What you place on your walls is as creative and as telling as the strokes on the canvas. Wall art sends a strong message as to what you value: your relationship with your own creative ability; your financial situation; your relationship with your family-of-origin, your children or spouse; and your overall disposition and approach to life.

So what does it mean if you have nothing at all on your walls? In general, barren walls mean a lower level of chi. Whether they are barren because you think you cannot afford to buy anything (relationship to money), cannot decide what to hang (blocked creativity), or are waiting for something else to happen first (passivity), the result is the same. Your chi remains in an inactive state of potential and needs to be activated.

Selecting wall art. Choosing something for your walls is like building your CD collection or selecting books for your library; you are essentially designing your life by what you choose. Because what you place on your walls cannot help but reveal your inner values, strengths, and relationships, it provides a tremendous opportunity for manifestation, but can also create much fear of failure. This fear can keep people stuck with bare walls for years.

Most people know what they do not want before they can identify what they do want. Select a wall where you know you want to put something, and place whatever you can lay your hands on there. Pick something up at a garage sale or hang a sheet if you have nothing. The point is that, after you hang something there, your mind will begin to tell you what it is that you do want. You will hear something along these lines. "That is way too small, the piece is going to need to be at least 24 inches by 36 inches." Or, "I want brighter colors here." Or, "It needs to be subtle and something old to calm the room. I don't want to make a loud garish statement." Besides stimulating your mind, hanging something will also jump-start your chi. You will feel activated by the placement just because you got your energy moving again. Sometimes you need this type of chi boost before you have the resources necessary to make the difficult choices or paint the wall.

This painting of a receding staircase transports the viewer to a magical realm.

Children often make the best artists. This owner enlivened her corner with a totem pole of decorated ceramic cups made by her child's art class.

Setting up a living space

If you have read a few feng shui books, you probably have quite a long list of what you should do in your space, but feel a bit overwhelmed as to how to make it all happen. Relax. No one can follow every feng shui rule in every room, and to try to do so usually leaves you with a room that feels contrived and ill-suited to your actual needs. This chapter will take you through the process of setting up a living room using feng shui principles, and help you to understand the sequencing behind the finished result.

Before feng shui

Originally, my client had placed the couch in front of the window in order to reserve the solid wall for the TV. Unfortunately, this placed the TV directly opposite the fireplace. This placement created a strong line of chi energy between the fireplace and the TV and divided the room in half. The couch in front of the windows also weakened the chi of the window, which was the most beautiful feature of the room, and weakened the chi of anyone sitting on the couch, since cold air seeped through in the evenings.

Stage one—begin with an empty room

To begin, you must empty the room of furniture in order to feel what is happening before you add any of your "stuff." Decide first how you will use the room; then, place the furniture. In this case, the dark brown wall color made the room feel like a tomb and the lack of light left the owner feeling depressed and sluggish in the winter. Although the owner wanted to lighten things up, she was worried about losing her grounding, since she tended to move very quickly through life, taking on one project after another and never completing them. She liked the size of the room, and did not want it to feel too formal.

The original couch placement blocked the windows, diminishing their beauty and ability to energize the room.

Based on the previous information, my client and I made the following decisions:

- We selected a light wall color that was also warm and earthy. This way the light could bounce and move through the room, but the owner still felt safe, stable, and grounded in the space. We created a custom gold with hints of green that has enough pigment to hold chi in the space, yet is light enough to allow easy movement and chi flow.
- We chose window treatments that allowed the light in. The light must penetrate as far into the room as possible, so we needed something that could be up and completely out of the way during the day. We selected natural bamboo Roman shades that allow light in and give a view of the nearby park. The bamboo keeps the room feeling earthy and in touch with natural forces.
- We removed anything artificial. The plastic ceiling medallions felt both artificial and too formal. The owner likes the light fixtures, so she simply removed the medallions above them.

Stage two—enter the primary players

With the room painted and ready to go, it was time to place the largest, most troublesome pieces in the room to get a sense of how large they were and possible placements.

We started with the rug, the TV, the couch, and a reading chair. I asked the owner how she intended to use this furniture. Who would sit where and what functions must each piece support? She wanted the rug/floor space to stay open so that she could perform her Pilates™ workout here without having to move things. The couch will serve many functions, including reading with her son in the evening, casual entertaining, chats with friends, snuggling with her husband while watching the news at night, and glancing at people out the window during the day. The chair will be used for reading and as a place for her to come and sit by herself. She uses this area both first thing in the morning and late at night.

- With the rug laid out, the couch was the first placement. Since no one always gets to have everything necessary for perfect feng shui in their home, we worked out a solution that at first "seemed" contradictory, yet in reality works quite well.
- We placed the couch on the solid wall facing the fireplace, restoring the fireplace as the room's designated focal point.

The decision to place the couch against the solid wall restored the room's focal point and provided a solid wall behind sitting areas.

Once these placements were made, it was easy to place the additional objects. The two large plants were positioned in front of the windows to both hold the chi in the room and to frame the center window. This left the intake vent open and allowed for better air circulation. The owner's prize original artwork was hung over the fireplace, since this area was now the uncontested focal point. Other plants and small tables filled in the corners and provided spots to set down drinks and books.

- The TV was next. Since the rest of the room was all windows or open to the adjacent dining room, we angled the TV in the corner of the room, subduing its presence while giving the owner a prime viewing alignment from the newly positioned couch. Although the TV covered part of the side window, the placement allowed chi to flow behind it so that it did not cut the windows off from the rest of the room the way the couch had.

- The chair needed to be segregated. However, it must be close enough that someone sitting in it could also see the TV and join in the conversation when desired. We angled it on the other side of the fireplace, complementing the angle of the TV and drawing the energy of the room toward the center.

With the couch gone from the window, we needed the plants to keep the chi force inside the room. Otherwise, the pull from the park across the street was too great.

Stage three—supply what is missing

When you move from house to house, you rarely have just what you need in order to make things work in the new space. Oftentimes rooms are larger than in the previous house (as with families who are moving from starter homes to larger family homes). However, sometimes they are smaller (as with reduced family size or other events require downsizing).

In this particular home, the new living room was larger than the previous one. The rug felt too small for the new space and people sitting on the couch seemed to yell across the room to the person sitting in the chair. The two sides of the room were still not connecting, resulting in stilted conversation. The space lacked the cozy feel of their previous smaller living room. It needed something, but what?

Without something in the center, the sides of this room pull apart, the chair and couch are too far away from each other, and conversation will be more difficult.

Adding plants in front of this window and at each corner of the room anchored a similar room and prevented the chi from escaping out the front window.

- The square ottoman could be used by both the person sitting in the chair and anyone sitting on the couch, whereas a typical coffee table or a rectangular ottoman could be reached only by someone on the couch. People now tend to lean in toward the center of the room and connect with each other, since the ottoman/table is the new place for drinks, magazines, etc.
- The ottoman/table is quite lightweight and easy to move, which makes it possible for the owner to slide it over and continue her Pilates in the room.
- The dark brown color grounds the center of the room (balancing out the large front windows), contains the chi flow, and revitalizes the space.
- The square shape, besides being another grounding influence, makes it easy to walk around all four sides of the piece without feeling blocked or constricted.

When moving from a smaller space to a larger one, add plants. Their life force will fill the larger room and eliminate the need to purchase additional furniture.

Adding the ottoman brought both sides of the room together and increased the social nature of the room. With coasters and a serving tray to protect its surface, it acts as a coffee table.

- The only lamps in the room were across the room from the reading area, making it awkward to use lamplighting without overhead lighting. The living room and dining room were energetically lopsided, because the pull of the park view was considerably stronger than any view in the dining room.

- The final addition was actually placed in the dining-room area that opened into the living room. A large horizontal mirror was hung on the dining-room wall facing the park. The mirror brought all the colors and beauty of the park into the dining room, and also activated the entire space between the front living-room window and the rear dining-room wall. This brought the two rooms back into balance and left everyone who entered feeling vitalized and energetic.

Each room has its own trouble spots. Maybe your troubles include floor radiators or a room with too many doors. Whatever is making it difficult for you, remember to position things according to how you and your family want to use the space, rather than by rules in a book. You will notice all these changes were made to balance out and support the needs, tastes, and tendencies of the family members who live in the space. Feng shui is not a list of dos and don'ts to be strictly applied. It is a process of understanding how the structures and patterns of a physical space impact the people who live and work there. Once you see how your home is influencing your interactions, you can shift your home to support your life.

The mirror above the sideboard reflects the adjoining room and connects them visually.

In this case, we did not solve the problem by focusing on just the living room. We had to look to an adjoining room for the answer.

Room for one

All man's miseries derive from not being able to sit quietly in a room alone.
—Pascal

Time alone—it petrifies some of us and comforts others. Regardless of how you feel about spending time alone, you will probably acknowledge that no one can be comfortable in the presence of others until one can be comfortable alone. Said a different way, others will be more comfortable in your presence when you spend time with you.

Creating comfort in alone spaces

"Make yourself at home" is a phrase we commonly use when guests come to visit. However, what does it mean to make yourself at home? What does it mean to be "at home" at all? For me, being at home is being comfortable in my own skin. Universally, it means knowing ourselves, liking ourselves, and accepting all of who we are. Alone spaces are vital in this process of knowing, liking, and accepting the self. A room for one opens the necessary space for internal reflection, exploration, and play. When you have your own space, you can feel what it is to "be you." Without this space, many of us are left wondering just who we are.

The bathtub is an ideal place to spend time alone. Taking just a moment to light a few candles, add essential oils, and include bath salts can make this time sacred.

Encouraging time alone

Depending on your five-element composition, you may have a problem spending time alone. People with either high-Wood or high-Fire energy have difficulty sitting still and being by themselves. Your reason for avoiding alone time should govern the creation of your private space.

Adding bamboo to any room is a simple way to make Wood energy feel at home.

Still unable to settle your Wood? Give yourself a green chair to sit in. Since Wood energy is drawn to green, you will be more likely to sit down. Prop your feet up on a footstool and wrap your legs in a blanket to give yourself that bit of extra enticement to stay seated.

Overcoming Wood's tendencies. If you have a lot of Wood energy, you need to be doing something all the time—even when you are alone. No problem. Set up alone spaces that allow for solitary activities such as fly tying, knitting, or charting your next vacation. The shower or bath is also a great place for you to be alone. The downward moving Water energy helps drain your excessive Wood and allows your busy mind and body to relax. Consider making evening baths your daily meditation.

Finding Fire's way. Fire energy is not at all interested in a day of solitude. In fact, being alone is Fire's greatest fear. Fire wants to merge and expand and, most of all, share. The best way for Fire to become comfortable with being alone is to view this as a preparation time for future sharing. If you have a lot of Fire, spend your first few "alone" hours in creative expression of your gifts and dreams. Make a collage or try painting a watercolor. Over time, you will begin to find that you have more to share with others socially because you have spent time with yourself.

This space might be overwhelming for some, but Fire energy finds itself through artistic expression, rather than through internal reflection. Colorful fabrics might be the only way to get Fire to take a seat.

Incorporating altars

An altar is a means of focusing your energy on particular connections. Spiritual altars focus this energy on your relationship with the divine; however, altars need not necessarily be about a connection with the divine, but they are meant to lift spirit.

48

The spiritual altar. The most common form of altar is a spiritual altar. This type of altar holds objects that help the individual feel personally connected to the divine. Although religious icons are common for this type of altar, any object that represents a personal connection will strengthen the energy of that connection. Think beyond the canned associations of your religious upbringing. What places in nature have inspired the "awe" of the divine in you? What objects inspire moments of personal reflection and internal exploration? What items remind you of your life's purpose and your connection to spirit through that sense of purpose? Use these items to build a personal altar that stirs your soul and comforts your heart every time you look at it.

The community altar. This type of altar was created by a group of feng shui practitioners who come together once a year to share in the energy of community. The altar was assembled by each person bringing an object that represented universal life force to them. After the energies of these objects had been joined through ritual, the individuals who took them home at the end of the retreat brought the energy of the entire group home, as well as their object. You can use community altars to draw the supportive loving chi of a group of friends into your home.

You can make an altar anywhere. This goddess figure and a small candle can transform a kitchen counter into sacred space.

A bathroom shelf dedicated to communion with the divine can "altar" the energy field of the entire house.

Traditionally, altars were made from religious icons. This Virgin Mary blesses all who enter here.

The travel altar. People from many cultures, such as Tibet, took personal altars with them when they traveled. These altars were usually an icon wrapped with incense in a cloth. Consider making a travel altar that will allow you to bring the energy of home with you whenever you spend time away. Items that hold energy, such as rocks, strips of cloth, or incense sticks, make good travel altars.

The nature altar. This form of altar is sometimes called a nature sanctuary. It is a place on your land that you set aside for the nature spirits and devas. By definition, this altar is not man-made. Rather than "creating" a nature altar, ask the nature spirits what place in your yard they would like to have as their own. Keep this area untouched, allowing things to grow wild. You might even want to put up a decorative border to let others know that this special place is off limits and should not be touched by humans. You will find that devoting a portion of your space to nature opens a respectful partnership between yourself and natural forces that will benefit your life in many ways.

Untouched land becomes a nature sanctuary and a tribute to nature's beauty and balance.

Shared spaces

50

A couple's space can be any room. What sets it apart are design elements intended to help two individuals open and share themselves. If you design the space correctly, vulnerable moments can feel safer, heated exchanges can soften and mellow, and cold shoulders can turn into a loving embrace.

A striking combination of feminine softness and masculine strength, this room represents and supports both the masculine and feminine partner. The carved wooden chair next to the plush softness of a slouchy ottoman generates its own yin/yang dynamic, while the paired containers connote a strong coupling. Additionally, some traditional plaid patterns are a complementary combination of yin and yang.

What is wrong with romantic spaces?

If all the "couple spaces" in your home are soft and romantic, that is a good thing, right? Not if one person in the partnership has a strong masculine essence. Essentially what we think of as "romantic" means yin, the feminine side of the partnership. Soft lights, soft colors, soft music, soft textures—it is all yin. These spaces are necessary, since they bring out and support the feminine partner's essence, but they cannot dominate every couple encounter. (Why do you think most masculine "guys" hang out in the garage instead of in the beautifully decorated soft-flowing living room?)

I would wager that some, if not most, feminine partners would love it if their masculine partner showed more strength, more direction, and more raw primal desire. The feminine partner needs a strong masculine essence in order to fully relax and begin the dance of the feminine. The stronger and more intensely present the masculine partner is, the more completely the feminine partner can experience her flowing gracious nature. But—here is the catch—you cannot expect a strong masculine person to hang out all day in a soft frilly house. That environment will not activate his yang chi force.

Having a hard time figuring out how to make your bedroom peaceful, romantic, and still represent the masculine? How many bedroom sitting areas have you seen that feel like a five-year old's tea party? This bedroom is a lovely restful blend of masculine and feminine, using the energy of two very different yet matching chairs to pull it all together.

Give a guy a leather chair and he is bound to stick around longer.

Use leather. Tried and true, a yang person likes leather. Whether leather activates his primal hunting gene, or some other brain chemical, experience has shown he will be more aggressive on a leather couch than on a couch decorated with a cotton floral print. If you would like to encourage a little more primal play with your partner, add leather.

Incorporating objects that your partner loves will increase his comfort level in the home.

Home cures

What can you do at home? Even though he may not spend as much time at home as you do, he will have a place to land if you incorporate his nature in the home.

Use decor items that represent action and movement. Baseballs, airplanes, and fast cars are all great choices. It is not just that they are traditionally "guy" things, it is that they are fast, and yang chi likes to flow quickly.

Incorporate plaids or squares within squares. The masculine likes to find and emphasize the edge. Although squares are a yin shape, when you put them together in a plaid, they become a symbol of the mathematical, systematic mind. Plaids are not just squares, they are components within a larger system, and any type of "systems thinking" is a masculine activity. Just try wearing a plaid shirt and see how feminine you feel.

De-clutter. I know sometimes it is his "stuff" and not yours that is filling every inch of floor space. However, regardless of whose clutter it is, the more stuff there is in a room, the slower the chi moves. Every stack of paper, every shelf full of knickknacks, all make the room more yin. This is truly a case of less is more—less stuff creates more yang.

53

A concrete wall lends raw strength to this bedroom, making it a place the masculine would love to frequent. The lamp, pillows, and plants keep it soft enough to appeal to the feminine partner, as well.

At first blush this bedroom comes across as soft and feminine, yet the masculine influence is unmistakable. How many yang identifiers can you spot?

- Minimal window coverings
- Pictures hung in a straight line
- Gym bag in corner by chair
- Riding cap on bench and boots on floor, indicating activity
- Blunt edges on footboard and headboard
- Busy pattern in rug
- White sheets

According to Christopher Alexander in *A Pattern Language*, ". . . a setting that is full of chairs, all slightly different, immediately creates an atmosphere that supports rich experience; a setting which contains chairs that are all alike puts a subtle straitjacket on experience."

The yin and yang of it

Of primary concern is that both individuals are represented in the space. Nothing shuts a person down faster than to not feel represented in his or her environment. Oftentimes, it is the feminine partner who sets up the couple's entire realm and then wonders why the masculine partner wants nothing to do with it. If a space does not hold enough masculine (what we have been calling "yang") chi, the masculine partner will not feel at home or supported by the space. Since the feminine partner is probably designing and setting up the space, she will need to work with her partner to bring his chi into the room. To create a couple's realm, both partners need to have a say in color selection, furniture selection, and wall decor. Even if he insists he does not care, he will respond better in the space if his needs are considered during the design phase.

Unmatched furniture. Every chair and pillow need not match. In fact, mismatched chairs make it easier for individuals to locate a place in the room that suits them and fits their body. Since women are typically smaller than men, the same chair that feels comfortable to a woman will not support a man. If everything in the space matches, chances are it is suiting only the person who designed it and not accommodating anyone else.

Different moods also require different styles and sizes of chairs. If all your chairs are the same size, what happens when you are in a mood to stretch out and relax vs. curl up into a tight ball?

The photographs in this section were taken to show how messages are communicated through furniture and design. After reading the captions for each photo, think about what kind of caption you would write for each couple's area in your home. Arrange your spaces to invite many more spontaneous moments for two.

The invitation

With the unlimited demands on a person's time today, time together as a couple does not often happen unless it is planned. Unfortunately, it is often spontaneous moments of laughter and sharing that make lasting memories. Cheer up. How you design your room can actually encourage both you and your partner to be more spontaneous. Think of your space design as an invitation. What is it inviting you to do? Do all your seating areas face the TV and not each other? Are your backyard lounge chairs facing the neighbor's garage? Is your bathtub big enough for two? Does your kitchen have enough room for two cooks, instead of one? Do you have pictures up of the two of you interacting in a loving, kind way?

Quiet reflection. **With a serene view of the lake and one chair curved slightly toward the other, this sitting arrangement whispers, "Join me for a moment of quiet reflection."**

Carefree and fun. The fun tropical prints and Mediterranean colors in this sitting area say: "Let's get away somewhere where there's no phone and no family responsibilities."

Wild and wonderful. Your wild side is sure to come out with these daring pillow covers. "Leave your inhibitions at the door!" is the unspoken message here.

Old reliable. Functional and practical, this arrangement is too far away from the fireplace to invite intimacy and the glass and metal table will squelch any spontaneous fun. Its message is more one of cooperation and camaraderie than intimacy and passion. It says, "I'll be here for you when you need my help."

A gathering place—group interactions

Coming together in community is a fundamental human need. In Joseph Campbell's highly acclaimed book, *The Hero with a Thousand Faces*, every life journey begins and ends in community. If you can create a space in your home where people feel accepted, loved, and included, you have performed a great service in the world. Communities come together around common causes. Your common cause might be the same parents or a shared love for jazz. As we all have numerous interests and communities in which we participate, you will have to select your primary communities and keep them in mind when setting up your home's gathering spaces.

Begin with the center in mind. Living rooms and family rooms devoid of the grounding and centering form of a coffee table do not get used. Why is this object in the center so important? In a gathering space, you need to pull disparate energies together and get them to interact. Your central table, ottoman, trunk, or stool accomplishes this by serving as the hub to which the various sitting spokes are attached. This does not mean you are limited to the standard coffee table with a stack of books on top. The following photos illustrate different ways in which to anchor a gathering place.

No stuffy table here. This home owner selected two architectural capitals to create a stunning, as well as grounded, family room.

To balance the ominous weight of the fireplace, this room demanded a large, heavy, stable center. The growing orchids on the table help lift this heaviness, adding some yang life force to an otherwise yin setting.

Try a coffee cart instead of a coffee table. Create your own coffee table out of a novel family heirloom or a yard-sale item. Such pieces appeal to the fun-loving side of us and encourage families to play more together.

Low to the ground, this traditional coffee table needed to be quite large to reach and anchor the different sitting areas around it. Had this table been smaller, the room would not have held together and each sofa or pair of chairs would have felt discon-nected from the center core.

Think in terms of circles

A gathering place needs to wrap around its members and hold them in a circular embrace. Circles represent community energy in numerous cultures including Native American and Asian. It strengthens feelings of inclusion and eliminates separateness. So how do you get the energy in the space to wrap?

62 **Curve seating arrangements.** Chairs seated side by side in a nice straight line might pass an army inspection, but they will not make your guests feel like talking to each other. If your furniture is already curved in shape, this point is not as dire. However, for furniture with straight backs and arms, introducing a curve through placement will soften their lines and encourage circular chi motion. Another rule of thumb: Pull furniture out a few inches from the wall and allow chi to circulate behind each piece.

Fill your corners. Empty corners drain energy from the center. Until the corners are full, the center will not feel supported. A carefully placed plant, a pair of five-foot iron candleholders, or a large basket filled with dried bamboo can relieve the stress on the room's center.

This white chair was lost against the white wall. By adding the active red screen, the chair immediately comes to life, beckoning the owner to sit down and snuggle up. As interesting as the screen is, its strongest function in the space is how it wraps energy around the back of the chair.

Implement circular decor items. Circular lamps, rugs, serving bowls, vases, wall art, and tables, all send the subconscious a message of inclusion. Rings (such as a candle with an enclosing candle ring) and wreaths have been used for centuries to signify that even strangers are welcome and that no one is excluded. If you make your wreath out of natural organic materials, it also symbolizes your connection to the seasonal patterns of the natural world and broadens community to include nonhuman forces.

This natural fir wreath brings the entire stairwell to life, welcoming all who enter. It has marvelous kinetic energy in its whorling branches.

Diversity is the key

Use different-sized chairs. Invite three people over and you will likely have three very different body types in your living room. If each person has to fit into the same size and shape of chair, chances are one or two might be too high, too low, too small, or too soft to be comfortable. Opt for an assortment of chairs, varying the size, shape, and softness of each. The comfort factor of your room increases exponentially.

You can bet the child who sits in this green mini Adirondack chair knows he is an accepted, integral part of the family. Make a place for your children as you would for your guests, and they will show up and participate more actively in family interactions.

Incorporate a variety of textures. Just as different-sized chairs increase a sense of comfort and inclusion, multiple textures can also scintillate your guests. A combination of plush carpeting, a linen sofa, and rattan chairs stirs the senses and accommodates the tactile needs of a broad consortium. Try mixing ultramodern textures, such as concrete and crafted steel, with natural components, like jute fibers and carved wood. Shiny silver candlesticks glow even brighter reflected in a rustic wooden mirror, and a silk wall hanging is certain to stand out against a stucco wall.

Cluster three or more together. Whether you are referring to chairs, candles, or coffee-table books, clusters form group energy. When the eye registers a grouping, it expands to "take it all in." Single objects tend to contract the eye (and your chi) in order to focus more fully on that one object.

Although a modern material, the cement wall has been imprinted with a wood-grain texture, which creates a primitive feeling.

Even in this minimalist setting, the owner has clustered seating to generate stronger group energy.

64

Removing window treatments opened this small living area and revealed a stunning view.

When your gathering place is too small

Use open furniture. Unless you are using a furniture piece to provide storage, keep your selections open and airy so that they do not stop the eye. If you can "see through" a piece, its energetic impact is considerably less than solid pieces.

Use vertical movement. If you cannot spread out, move up. If your ceilings are at least eight-feet high, use vertical positioning to create movement for the eye and to lessen the stuck feeling that can settle into a small space. Caution: Avoid placing too many items on furniture or on shelves above your head. Instead of increasing a feeling of freedom, items hanging above the head feel oppressive and threatening.

Minimize window treatments. Heavy drapes will cause the chi to sink. Use vertical coverings or no covering at all to open the space.

Enlarge doorways and openings. Placing decorative items (such as potted plants) on the sides of a doorway can expand the chi of the door, creating more yang movement in the space.

Introduce more living plants. During the day, living plants constantly generate chi, reducing the strain on the human element to fill the space. Emotionally, your home will feel less demanding and more supportive.

By adding a few small tables, an arrangement of flowers and a basket, this large room becomes more compact.

Size matters

A group gathering is intimately affected by the size of the room. Just as Goldilocks discovered when she went to visit the three bears, group gathering places can be too large, too small, or just right. If yours is just right, lucky you. If not, the following information will give you some tips on how to grow or shrink your space to fit the size of your group.

When your gathering place is too large

Large open spaces seem ideal, but they can drain life force from humans if there is not enough chi present in the surroundings themselves. In a large room, you will have to work harder to make others feel comfortable and included in what is going on.

Increase furniture density. Obviously the more you fill your space with furniture and decor items, the less "empty" space there is. Be careful not to line your walls and leave the center of your space empty. (See lower photograph on page 67.)

Watch furniture size. Nothing makes a place feel larger than small furniture items. You are much better off having fewer larger pieces than a bunch of small occasional tables or single chairs. Furniture that blocks a view of the wall behind it and the floor beneath it is much more stabilizing in a large space than tables with open legs or shelving that is open to the wall behind it. Open furniture pieces are best in small places.

Too much open space in the center. Connect sitting areas that are further than four feet apart by opting for an L-shaped sofa or adding an ottoman. Central objects allow for a common focal point that connect people to each other.

The ottoman grounds the center of the room, providing a common horizontal surface for all the seating areas.

Add pictures of people. Adding photographs of loved ones, friends, or deceased family members can help you energetically fill a room that would otherwise be too large.

This large room is functionally cozy. Here is what makes it work:

- Numerous photographs of family, friends, and travel fill the back table, bringing life to what could otherwise be a dormant area.

- The dark low window edge complemented by the fold in the drapes draws a horizontal line around the room, bringing the energy down to the seating level. This horizontal line also keeps the chi in the room from escaping into the ocean beyond the windows.

- The large L-shaped sofa fills an entire corner. This single piece is much more grounding than scattering numerous small chairs around the room would be.

- The warm earth tones draw energy inward and hold it still, another calming yin feature of the space.

- The variety of textures—smooth wood, supple leather, chenille throw, silk drapes—activate the senses and keep an active energy exchange going throughout the room.

- The strong border around the edge of the rug pulls the room in. The border is more than two feet wide, which draws the items inside it even closer together.

Use five-element balancing

People feel included in a community when they are somehow represented in the space. An easy and highly successful way to represent any possible combination of people is to bring aspects of each of the five elements into your gathering place. No matter what type of person walks through your door, they will have something "in common" with the space through this elemental bond.

Earth

Earth likes to be at the center of a gathering. Include an ottoman or coffee table. Use square shapes.

Earth feels safe low to the ground and with soft comfy cushions or throws handy.

Earth wants to sit next to someone else, not be seated alone, and is happy to hold a serving tray or play bartender.

Let your earth guests "help out," (select music, mix drinks, chop vegetables).

Add containers to your gathering space to increase Earth's comfort.

Social Activities for Earth:
- Hold a cooking class in your home in which everyone makes a part of the meal and then enjoys it together.
- Have a quilting bee to provide activity, a creative outlet, and some easy conversation.

Metal

Metal will not relax with cat hair on the couch or dirt on the windows. Nothing distracts metal more than clutter or disarray. Tidy up more than you might otherwise.

Metal needs open space to breathe and prefers minimal furniture.

Is there a corner or a room that could benefit from less?

White trim and white ceilings and monochromatic flower arrangements help Metal feel comfortable.

Metal's gift is how to tell the excess from the essential.

Social activities for Metal:
- Gather a group for spring cleaning or closet clearing. Take turns showing up at each others' houses to deep clean or sort. Metal figures out what to keep and what to throw away.

Water

Water needs but resists social interaction.

Cascading plants or organic flowing shapes will help Water feel at ease.

Give Water a place to sit off by himself with space for just one or two others. An away room just off the hall from the larger social center was invented just for Water.

Social activities for Water:
- Hold a monthly group yoga session or meditation circle in your home. The group energy will build and the vibration will rise. As a group, you will actually have insights and experiences that would be more difficult to attain by yourself and Water's underlying need for connection will be filled.

Wood

Wood, a natural leader and outgoing personality, takes over your gatherings if you let him.

Wood people get things rolling. They are always involved in new projects and up on the latest ideas/trends/developments.

Include Wood by planning activities as part of your social encounters.

Wood ancestors raised a barn or helped bring in a neighbor's crop. Have something to do in your gathering place.

Live plants and tall vertical objects will encourage Wood to join the group.

Social activities for Wood:
- Share a book of French phrases or a wine tasting.
- Bring a group together to build something to serve them all, such as a neighborhood sled run or a community garden.
- Create team obstacle courses or word games, community house painting projects, or neighborhood leaf raking.
- Make jewelry or style scrapbook pages.

Fire

Having more than one person in a room draws Fire like a magnet.

Activate Fire with triangular shapes and diamond patterns.

Activate the senses, crank up the intensity, open Fire's heart.

Make people laugh to delight Fire. Social times allow other folks get to know and enjoy the presence of Fire.

Encourage Fire with candles, music, alcohol, food, flowers, textures, art, and dancing.

Social activities for Fire:
- Throw a dance jam for adults and children. Have one dance jam featuring a new music style every month: tango or square dancing followed by improv.
- Ask talented folks to teach the rest or get a video.
- Enjoy an evening of Japanese flower arranging or take a wildlife photography class.
- Take turns deciding on what the class will be.

Find that element

This entry hall is a classic balance of all five elements, making it an easy space to greet formal visitors as well as intimate friends. (Remember the elemental nature of an object is discerned by its color, shape, and material.)

- ■ Earth: square pictures hung in a horizontal line, cream wall color
- ■ Metal: white round Chinese vase, white round pots for plants, metal table stand, clean orderly feeling, gray matting in pictures
- ■ Water: cascading plants, black table base with glass tabletop in hallway, privacy aspect of the sliding door (provides more privacy for eating area, which water needs to feel comfortable)
- ■ Wood: tall carved Chinese doors, statues on top of interior wall that raise the eye to the same height as the carved doors, vertical panels in the dining room, hardwood flooring, pillar shapes in table base
- ■ Fire: triangular pendulum in table base, red rugs, track lighting to spotlight objects in the evening, brightly colored flowers on the dining table, diamond patterns in the rug

The formal living room

74 Tradition plays a strong role in formal living rooms, symbolizing your link to your ancestral past. Living rooms are more-formal spaces than family rooms, and have their own story to tell. Your formal living room is your connection to ancestral energy patterns. Rooted in tradition, the items displayed in your living room reveal your family-of-origin's imprint on your current reality. Our link to the past determines how safe we feel in the present. This living room holds several past-generation items:

- iron mantel brought from the ancestral home,
- wall scrolls that depict the family's history,
- refinished chairs from a prior generation,
- antique wall hangings, trunk, and drum tables,
- family kimono.

The family room

The family room or its cousin, the great room, allows for a psychological separation between the ancestral family and the immediate family. The relaxed nature of a family room or great room gives you the space to play and explore, trying out different ways of interacting than you might have grown up with. Family rooms and great rooms often function as the mingling zones, the places where family members come together after exiting their private spaces (bedrooms and offices). As such, the family room needs to hold objects that relate to each family member.

Once every member has adequate "representation," you can work on adding layers of functionality that will combine to make this room a place that does indeed bring your family together. This room holds:

- the husband's favorite wall art,
- the husband's CD collection,
- the wife's cozy throw,
- a child's favorite reading book.

Avoid computers in this room. Family rooms are for interactions. Usually, the type of family interaction that happens surrounding a computer is arguing over turns. Computers encourage people to tune into a virtual reality, rather than work to enhance their actual reality. The computer is now the source of more "couple" fights than any other piece of electronic equipment in the house, including the television.

Family rooms that inhibit movement train people to be passive. This passivity can extend to numerous areas of a person's life. If you want your children to be actively involved in making their life decisions, give them the space to move and explore.

Play together. What kind of play does your family engage in? Do you pull out a chess set or play the piano? Do you tell stories or wrestle on the floor? Whatever form of family play suits you, make certain you have the space, the toys, or the props you need to entice interest at a moment's notice.

Invite neighbors and friends into this space often. Help young ones know that their family-of-origin relates harmoniously with larger social patterns. If no one but the family is ever in the family room, children do not get to see how their family fits into the larger social picture.

Color matters. This is not the place for a white-on-white color scheme. Use child- and spill-friendly colors and make certain that at least 60 percent of the colors in the room are warm tones. (See Which colors are safe? on pages 114–116.)

Lamplighting. Soft light encourages more intimate conversation, but be certain it is bright enough that people can see the expressions on each others' faces. Much of our communication happens through facial expressions, rather than through spoken words. Candles added to lamplight sprinkle magic throughout family moments and energetically bond family members together.

This relaxed room invites family fun. The ottoman on wheels can be rolled away to open the center, allowing room for wild and rambunctious children to play.

Include a mantel. A mantel is not only an important focal point, it is a strong indicator of ability to attract chi. Linked to the ancestral hearth, a fireplace does not need to be lit to attract chi. An interesting and purposeful mantel arrangement can bring the energetic patterns of various shapes to work for you, gathering chi. Empty fireplaces should be avoided at all costs, since they represent dormancy and the inability to bring potential possibilities into the realm of the actual.

The reverse triangle created by these two horses set amidst the wall sconces is a way of directing power (chi force) down from heaven into the house.

The environmental interior

It is not hard to imagine yourself on safari when you walk into this sitting room. Palm trees, antelope-patterned rug, tropical-print chaise lounge, and bamboo chairs all work together to bring this adventurous room to life.

There are many ways of bringing the powerful influence of nature indoors. Regardless of whether or not you enjoy a year-round porch, you can select one of your favorite places in nature as a decorating theme. When you create an interior tribute to the seashore, a pine forest, or a woodland meadow, you create a home space that resonates with a particular natural environment. The effect is more than visual. Your home's frequency alters. If selected as your theme, the jungles of the rain forest, for example, would influence your senses, thought patterns, and emotional responses. The truer you are to your natural source of inspiration, the stronger this energetic link will be. For many it is a sacred connection.

Capture color

The strongest visual and vibratory link to your natural environment is color. Even with no ocean view, a periwinkle/white combo invites the seashore into your home while fuchsia pink lands you in the middle of a tropical island. The warm glow of terra-cotta walls can recall a walk down a path of sun-baked earth, and celadon green holds the allure of an Asian dynasty.

The color-capturing process is where all your magazine reading can come in handy. Rip out pictures of places that resonate with your theme and match them up with paint chips. Try buying quarts of various "theme" colors and mixing them on the wall, layering your gold over your green until you get just the right hue. This eliminates the stress of painting the entire room only to realize that your "palladian blue" looks mint green or that a soft violet turned gray. Once you get just the right color mixed on your wall (and in your paint tray), dab a stir stick into the mixture and take it down to a paint specialist that hand-mixes color. Computer matching is rarely close enough for energy design.

Materials

Stone. As a bowl of pebbles, a heart-shaped stone next to an intimate photo, a rock garden, or a slab for a coffee table, stone enters the home in many ways. Cobblestone paths will teleport you all the way to old Europe, so why not use two cobblestones as bookends? If you pick up favorite rocks on a nature walk, add them to a zen sand garden for a dynamic effect. If river rocks are your favorite, why not refinish your family-room mantel with your private collection?

Tile. Mexico comes instantly to mind with its deep blue and terra-cotta tiles. France has its own tile style, opting for white-and-blue scrollwork or a crisp black-and-white check, and the red roofs of Spain strike even the casual visitor. Tile can hang on the wall like a photo, deck out your floor, or rest in a tabletop. A tile trivet works in the kitchen and tile borders can be added almost anywhere. Glazed tiles increase yang, adding movement to the room, whereas unglazed tiles are porous and absorbent, increasing yin.

Wood. Wood is one of the most fundamental building blocks of any environment and can take the form of a bark basket, a hollowed-out stump for a planter, a carved mirror frame, or an antique door. Avail yourself of wood and you capture the strength of its original location.

Wicker. This bending reed can take almost any shape, indicating flexibility and endurance. Wicker is also a strong summer signal (See Seasons on page 84.) and beach locator. It is hard to walk along a string of beach houses anywhere in the world and not see wicker in some form. No room for a wicker rocking chair? Try a floor basket or a small table.

82

This carved-wood table evokes a sense of faraway places. The wicker chair helps support the feeling that this room is a retreat from chaos.

Metal. Scrolls, braces, table legs, and lamps—metal is easy to add. Lending its edge to ancient civilizations as well as to modern lofts, metal provides the ability to define a space, carving out the area surrounding an object in order to add clarity. This clarity can feel sharp if overdone. Soften metal's sharp edges by surrounding it with an absorbent material such as wood.

Leather. Full of fire, leather brings the animation and life of the animal kingdom into a physical environment. It is no wonder that leather brings out the masculine life force in people, putting most men instantly at ease in a room. Leathers range from rough Montana cowhides to supple Italian pieces, with everything in between. Studded leather couches, pincushion stools, or coffee-table inlays, all increase the yang energy in a room as well as heighten sensitivity to touch.

Cut glass, like this round faceted crystal, can bring rainbow rays into the room.

Glass. What else can create rainbows on your wall, protect you from the eyes of prying neighbors, or allow you to feel the warmth of the sun on a winter's day? Glass is multifaceted. It can be transparent or opaque, thick or thin, clear or colored. A wall of glass block can modernize a blasé rambler with the updated feel of a city loft. An antique glass collection can land you back on an ancestral farm.

Woven fibers and textiles. A brilliant turquoise-blue pashmina throw from India can make any room feel exotic. This wonderful combination of silk and wool gets softer with every washing, and is as functional as it is beautiful. Old cottons, denims, or a patchwork quilt made from flannel pajamas will support your effort to create a rustic getaway, just as velvet is sure to come across as posh and luxurious. Woven fibers and textiles are as tactile as they are visual. Be certain to take into account what you will touch, as well as what you will see.

Scents

A powerful link, smell should be considered a part of your decorating scheme, rather than an afterthought. Every home has particular scents that are the accumulation of the various activities and objects in the home. Be certain to refresh sensory experiences often, keeping them in harmony with the seasons.

Seasons

Capture the best season of your selected environment. If you visit the Rocky Mountains during ski season, your tribute to this mountain environment should include a snowy landscape or antique wooden skis. If your trips to the seashore are your favorite summer outing, your seashore room might be painted the sandy color of driftwood bleached by the sun. Many furnishings have seasonal associations. Bamboo suggests the quick growth of spring, wicker evokes summer, a leaf motif recalls the fall, and leather summons winter. If the environment you are working with does not experience strong seasonal changes, you can still shift the color of your flowers, candles, or coverings to keep your home feeling alive.

The skis, plaid furnishings, and roaring fire bring back strong memories of a winter spent skiing in the Rockies.

Thematic objects

Let your travels be your guide. Environmental interiors are stronger if they link to a place you have personally experienced. It is nice to do the log cabin theme, but if you have never inhaled the crisp cold pine-scented air of a Rocky Mountain December or chopped wood for a morning fire, then your link to that environment will not be as strong. When selecting a theme, consider special childhood places, favorite romantic getaways, or travels to other cultures. If you were to sit down, close your eyes, and call up a "place in nature" that would make you feel both comfortable and alive; that place should be your theme environment. The objects should have a spiritual aesthetic that can breathe soul into the room.

Recreate your favorite vacation just by using colors and collected objects from the locale in your decor.

85

Priority placements

All you practical people reading feng shui books, this chapter is for you. The need for what I call "priority placement" feng shui shows up in those moments when you find yourself entertaining the thought of fresh-squeezed orange juice for breakfast, only to realize that the juicer is hidden in the back of your appliance cupboard. Too much effort. The urge recedes and you opt for the carton in the refrigerator. Had you placed the juicer in the front half of your cupboard, your experience might have been different. Another example of priority placement feng shui could find you unconsciously flipping on the TV when you get home, not because you want to watch what is on, but because it is the first thing you see when you walk through the door.

What is priority placement feng shui?

The priority placement approach recognizes that we humans typically expend as little time and energy as possible to get through the day. It is not likely that you will get the ladder out of the garage and use it to crawl up into the attic to get down the dishes for Sunday dinner. Items you need to use or places you need to attend to on a daily basis should be close by.

The need for priority placement feng shui was made painfully obvious to me when I moved into my current house. I was dumbfounded when I discovered that, after 100 years of use, no one had installed a phone jack on the main-living level. For the first week that I lived there, I ran up and down the stairs every time the phone rang, trying to remember whether I had left the phone on the charger. When I simply think of the combined energy expended by people running upstairs to answer the phone every day for the past 100 years, I am exhausted.

Make it easy on yourself. Before reorganizing, this formal living room arrangement blocked people from entering.

The new arrangement welcomes guests into the room and increases chi flow throughout.

Priority placement feng shui recognizes that we often opt for whatever action requires the least amount of effort.

—author

Working with priority placement feng shui

Working with practical feng shui is easy and offers immediate results. It follows the cardinal feng shui rule that you should set up your house as a model of the type of life you want to live. If everything in your home is handy and you can get what you need with ease and comfort, your life will reflect this ease. You first must decide what your priority-one goals are; then you can place the objects necessary to meet your goals in a priority-one location in your home. This process brings your inner intentions into alignment with your external surroundings.

Priority-one goals

Priority-one goals are the things you would like to be doing every day. If you were to imagine your ideal day, what would it contain? Would you spend the morning curled up in a chair reading? Meditating by yourself? Walking your dog in the park? Chatting over a cup of coffee? If so, you should have a book handy, or a meditation spot, or a park nearby, or coffee on hand. What would you do in the afternoon or the evening? How much of your day would be spent alone and how much time would be spent with other people? After you decide what your ideal day would be like, you will be ready to set up your priority-one areas.

Without a piece of service furniture to act as a handy gathering place near the entrance, items tend to pile up. The right entrance container will have a place for mail, letter openers, keys, cell phones, sunglasses, and wallets.

Priority-one areas

The places you go every day with little thought are your priority-one areas. These areas should house the most necessary items in the home. For example, the space between your parking spot and the door to your house is a priority-one area. Since you walk that 10–20 feet every day, put something there that needs your daily attention, such as a small vegetable garden. You could pull a ripe tomato or head of fresh lettuce every day after work as you walked into the house to fix dinner.

Over time, such placements will change the way you live. Set up your priority-one areas to represent and support your ideal life. Take a moment to think about what is located in the priority-one areas listed below and remove items from these areas that are not in harmony with your intentions or desired lifestyle.

Items placed on lower shelves would be considered in priority-one zones since these items will be at eye level.

- Area between your parking spot and where you enter your home
- Area surrounding your bed
- Bathroom sink
- Inside of the shower
- Area within reach of the toilet
- Kitchen sink
- Front of eye-level kitchen cupboards
- Refrigerator
- Stove or microwave
- TV viewing spot (couch, chair, or favorite floor position)
- Passageway between the kitchen and the TV area
- Passageway between the bed and the bathroom
- Passageway from your home office to the bathroom
- Area within reach while you are seated at your desk
- Garage or workspace that gets used every day

Priority-two goals

Priority-two goals are things you need or want to do every week, but that do not require daily attention. Do you want a clean house? Then you will need time and energy set aside for weekly cleaning. Do you want to socialize regularly with neighbors and friends? Then you will need areas set up for socializing. Think about your ideal week. Does it include one, two, three, or more nonworking days? Do you spend full days alone, sharing your space with others only once or twice a week? Are children present part of the time, all of the time, or none of the time? As the designer of your life, what will you include in your ideal week?

Formal dining rooms are considered priority-two areas if they are not used on a daily basis.

Priority-two areas

Priority-two areas are places that are easy to get to, but you do not go there without consciously deciding to do so. For example, you would not open a cupboard unless you wanted something inside it, and you would not walk into the sunroom unless you wanted to be there. Place items in priority-two areas that require your attention on a regular, but not daily, basis. For example, you might go out on the back porch every other day to check the sprinklers or water the lawn. In this case, the back porch would be a priority-two area. If you have a reading room that you enter once or twice a week, that room is a priority-two area. Common priority-two areas are listed below.

- The back porch (or front porch if you typically enter through a rear or side door)
- The front of your closet (even though this area is in the front, the closed door means you do not see this area unless you choose to open the door)
- The formal living room or dining room (assuming you do not use these rooms every day)
- Craft rooms or guest rooms that you enter occasionally
- A den or office that is used weekly but not daily
- A garage or workspace that gets used often, but not every day

Priority-three goals

Priority-three goals are projects you have consciously put on hold or tasks that require minimal effort from you (like an automatic sprinkler system). Priority-three goals are also seasonal, and may move up to priority one or priority two at certain times of year (such as decorating the house for Christmas or deep cleaning in the spring). However, most of the time, they are of lesser importance. When considering your priority-three goals, ask yourself what you want or need to do every year that makes each season more meaningful.

Priority-three areas

Priority-three areas require some effort to get to. If you place items there that you should but do not want to attend to, such as bills that need to be paid, you are sabotaging yourself. Move your bills into a priority-one area and it will be much easier to pay them. Priority-three areas are fine for hobbies or tasks that are not pressing or difficult. As you read through the list to the right, ask yourself whether the items in these areas are things you would seldom use in your ideal life or whether they should be moved to a more active area. For example, if your baking goods are stuffed to the back of a closet (a priority-three area), but ideally you would like to bake bread every day, you need to change the placement of your baking goods to support your life goals. Or, if you want to start a business (a priority-one goal), but your office is in a dark and cluttered basement (a priority-three area), consider moving your office up into the living room while you get things going. Otherwise, you will need to transform the priority-three basement area into a priority-one or -two space.

- Flower or garden bed at rear of property
- An unattached garage or shed that is seldom used
- The backs of cupboards
- The tops of closets
- The cupboard underneath the sink
- Any cupboard or container that needs to be unlocked before it can be opened
- The basement
- The attic
- An off-site storage area
- A place on your property that requires more than a five-minute walk to reach

Priority placements encourage you to know yourself, to focus on your intentions, and to set up your home so that it supports those intentions. Now that you know where priority one, two, and three areas are located, you can evaluate your placements to see exactly what you have made into the most important things in your life.

A matter of light

Light is one of the most powerful chi enhancers of all environmental elements. It represents consciousness and awareness. To understand something better is to "shed light on it" and to bring something "to light" means to become aware of its hidden, subconscious meanings. Light is also a powerful regulator of moods and physical body systems. To date, there have been more than 3,000 studies on the effects of light on human chronobiology (our internal rhythms and cycles activated or controlled by light.)

Plan for a comfortable balance between natural and controlled light.

One of nature's strongest yang forces, lighting affects everything else in the room. If the lighting is too diffused, for example, it prevents the eye from focusing easily on individual objects. This happens often with overhead florescent lights. On the other hand, lighting that is too dim generates a strong yin effect on the body, bringing on depression and dark moods. This chapter will focus on the following three factors to evaluate your home's lighting: color, illumination, and chi flow.

A floor filled with dappled sunlight recalls an intimate connection with the sun's force.

Color

Full-spectrum lighting. Full-spectrum lighting has received quite a bit of attention lately. Just about every major line of lightbulb manufacturer now produces a full-spectrum bulb. Just what is full-spectrum lighting good for? Full-spectrum lighting eliminates spikes in the color spectrum, thereby producing a more balanced white light. This means the colors you see in the items around you are true colors because the light itself is not absorbing more of one color ray than another. Your gold looks gold, not greenish gold, and your periwinkle wall is just that, periwinkle.

Why blue light might be better. As we age, the cornea hardens and yellows. Which means, everything we see gets more and more yellow. There are lightbulbs available now that adjust for the yellowing of the cornea and create a truer color representation. For anyone over the age of 60, lightbulbs with a blue bias are beneficial.

Color temperature. Another feature related to color is the temperature of the color ray. The Japanese have conducted research on the physiological responses to high and low color temperatures, and found that high color temperatures (the 5000–6000 Kelvin range) enlarge pupil size and allow more light to the retina. This means, with the right temperature light, you will need less illumination (See Illumination on page 93).

This hand-blown glass lighting fixture brings memories of a trip to Italy, as well as illumination, to this dining room.

Illumination

Illumination is most important in the winter when you do not get as much natural exposure to bright outdoor light. You need illumination, especially first thing in the morning, to keep your body's many chemical and emotional cycles in balance. One of the most documented imbalances caused by a lack of bright light is seasonal affective disorder (SAD). Discovered in 1980, SAD is triggered by the shorter daylight hours. The lack of light (illumination) allows the body's sleep signal, melatonin, to build up to higher than normal levels, which disrupts the body's daily sleep-wake cycle. When the sleep-wake cycle is disrupted, you feel the symptoms of jet lag:

- clinical sleep disorders,
- severe fatigue,
- major digestive problems,
- the inability to react or concentrate.

What is the best solution? As noted on page 92, full-spectrum lighting produces a more balanced white light, but does nothing to increase lux (the amount of illumination). It is the lack of brightness, not the color of the light that results in SAD. Additionally, you need that illumination at a particular time of day, especially early in the morning, because you have got to reset your internal clock. Your internal clock is a pair of very small organs in the brain called suprachaismatic nuclei (SCN). How it actually works is that the retina detects light, sends the signal to the pineal gland, then the pineal gland activates the SCN, which in turn tells the pineal gland to stop producing melatonin. That said, here are some effective measures for getting your biological clock back in sync.

A small reading lamp behind the couch adds much-needed light to this area during winter months.

- Light-boxes have been a highly recommended adjustment for SAD sufferers, however, they have limitations. For starters, you have to spend an hour every morning staring into a bright square of light (no wonder people try medication rather than spend their time this way). Also, some of the light-boxes do not have UV filters on them, which can damage the retina and skin.
- Light-visors have been proven just as effective as light-boxes, and do not require staring into a bright square of light for an hour every morning. The light does not need to be as bright because it is positioned closer to the retina. They also have UV filters.

Allow as much light as possible by opening your curtains and blinds, no matter which season reigns outdoors.

- I strongly recommend a simulated-dawn alarm clock (sometimes called a sunrise alarm clock), which simulates the sunrise and helps reset your body's internal clock.
- Resist the temptation to draw your curtains or blinds during winter months. Allow as much natural light in as possible.
- Get your windows cleaned regularly. A thin film of dirt can block up to 50 percent of your precious sunlight.
- Adjust your work schedule to allow for an hour outside every day during daylight hours (sunlight ranges from 10,000 to 100,000 lux, whereas a brightly lit office is only about 1,000 lux).
- If possible, add a skylight in an area of your home that does not receive as much natural light due to the lower placement of the sun in winter.
- Add incandescent lamps in rooms where you spend a lot of time.

This alarm clock simulates the rising sun, naturally awakening the body just as it finishes a rapid eye movement (REM) sleep cycle.

Using light to direct chi

Balanced light. Is balanced light a good thing? As mentioned earlier, when light becomes too diffused, i.e. too balanced, our ability to perceive individual objects diminishes. Diffused light also loses its ability to direct chi. In yin/yang theory, there must be places of darkness in order to comprehend places of light. Only through dimming areas of a room can other areas stand out. Allow for shadow, but use it artistically. Like the mat surrounding a well-framed painting, shadow can help you highlight a room's defining characteristics.

Identify sources of natural light. Light is a design variable that changes throughout the day and with the seasons. In the winter, the sun sits lower in the sky than during the summer, and of course, southern exposures will always be brightest during the middle of the day. Once you know how much natural light you have in different areas, you will know better how to supplement it with artificial sources.

- Identify the time of day you are most likely to be in a certain area (See Feng Shui Zones on pages 142–158 to work through this).
- Watch how the light changes throughout the day. Supplement with task lighting.
- Use window coverings that allow for variable lighting options.
- Think about the function of the space and how much light you need to work there. Some functions, such as making crafts or cooking, require general lighting. Other tasks, such as reading or tying flies, need localized task lighting.
- Once you know your needs, add task lighting in the form of lamps, spotlights, undercounter lights, or tracks for areas that support detailed work.

You can't have a light without a dark to stick it in. —Arlo Guthrie

Localized task lighting for leisure reading is ideally placed near your favorite chair.

Use lighting to identify focal points. For rooms with more than one focal point, or rooms without a strong focal point, use a spotlight or row of track lights to draw the eye to your designated center. Wherever light is strongest, that is where the eye goes first; everything else is secondary.

Lights should move up as well as down. Since lighting directs chi, sometimes you will need to move energy up a wall, as well as down. For wall lighting, your eye will focus on the fixture and move from there. If the fixture directs light upward, your eye and your chi will rise. If the fixture directs the chi downward, your eye and your chi will sink.

96 **Consider sconces such as those pictured below that direct light up as well as down to balance the space.**

Outdoor living spaces

A blur of green. The smell of grass. A profusion of color. Warm evening air. Outdoor environments have their own magic, their own finesse. To be outside is to interface with nature spirits and the souls of trees, as well as city streets and neighboring fences. Somewhere between the urban and the primitive, outdoor spaces open us and soothe us like no indoor space can.

Comfortable outdoor spaces evolve as you learn to interact with the natural forces that make up your landscape. Whether those forces include trees, boulders, hills, rich soil, clay, blue jays, or skyscrapers, you must create a relationship in which you communicate your needs to nature and learn to listen to her replies.

The constancy of change

Feng shui is the study of how the natural patterns of the environment interface with and affect human beings. The first thing to consider about an outdoor environment is that you necessarily give up quite a bit of control. You do not control the temperature, or whether it is intensely bright or dark and cloudy. You cannot keep pests away or airborne seeds. From the minute you wake up in the morning to the time you go to bed, your outdoor environment is changing. The more you plan for those changes, the easier it is to transform them into a source of enrichment rather than frustration.

I go to nature to be soothed and healed, and to have my senses put in order.
—John Burroughs

A comfortable outdoor environment is one that works with, not against, natural patterns and forces.

An outdoor trellis is a yin feature, adding elements of protection, shade, and support.

Tempering with yin and yang

Every day, the morning sun dries the dew from the grass, wakes up the birds, and floods the sky with color. The yang increases. Each evening sun pulls all those glorious colors back in, waves goodbye with a wink, and then it is gone. Yin increases. Yang's force is felt as spring pushes tender flowers up through crusty snow and summer blazes wilt flowers in a day. Yin's softening begins in the fall, toning everything back down, settling into the deep yin of winter. Outdoor designers must learn to balance the yin and yang shifts of nature to create spaces that allow us to enjoy a fullness of outdoor experiences. When the sun dims in the evening, the outdoor gazebo glows with twinkling lights. When the sun blazes white hot, we pull a stretch of canvas across a frame to create shade. We temper wind with trees, add rocks to create visual interest during winter, and find ways to keep flowers blooming from early spring to late fall.

Yin features. Yin garden features provide safety, shelter, and relaxation. They tend to decrease the human element and increase the natural element. For example, a garden bench overgrown with ivy would be more yin than the same bench in the center of a patio with no ivy in sight. Hanging plants are more yin than upright ones and any item that brings the eye or body down lower to the ground will increase yin. Yin surfaces are often soft and absorbent, since the nature of yin is to receive energy and hold it still.

Yang features. Yang garden features invite exploration, activity, and movement. They allow the sun free reign and provide plenty of reflective surfaces to keep the light bouncing. Bright colors, patterns, and dynamic shapes are all a part of yang's array. Harder surfaces will keep energy moving faster than absorbent ones, as will straight lines. And any upright vertical object such as a tall tree, birdhouse, or sundial keeps chi moving up and out in a yang pattern.

Adding a vertical object to an overgrown (and, therefore, "yin") flower bed area will increase yang.

Between haven and earth

A gradual transition between outside and inside is essential for harmony between your home and its surroundings. When grass runs directly to the walls of the house, the connection between earth and home is too abrupt. A transition space where outdoors and indoors mix is needed. Home owners without a transition space may feel cut off from the world, unable to connect intimately to family, friends, and nature.

- Shrubs, flower beds, and other forms of greenery should rise up to meet the house. Higher than the surrounding lawn, greenery will ground the house, making it feel safe and rooted in the earth. Without this semienclosure in Mother Earth, a house feels out of place, transplanted, and unsafe.

- A curved path to the house encourages visitors to slow their approach and shift more gradually from outdoors to in.
- Porches create the perfect interface; they function somewhat like a room, providing relief from sun and elements, and somewhat like a yard, full of plants, and sunshine.
- Rock gardens are great outdoor features for high-altitude environments that do not allow long growth cycles. Like shrubs or bushes, rocks can ground and stabilize a house, helping it feel solid, permanent, and safe.

This owner used rock quarried from the surrounding hillside, to link her yard to the grounding, stabilizing force of an entire mountain.

Protective porches

A porch is a wonderful potpourri of experience. Structurally, it represents shelter and protects one from exposure to the elements. By definition, a porch is a covered vestibule, but when the vestibule is uncovered, then it is not able to perform this protective function. You and your visitors will feel vulnerable. If your porch is exposed, place an item there that signals your willingness to care for yourself and your visitors. This could be a welcome sign, welcome mat, a bench to set items down on, or even a colorful pot of flowers.

Front porches. Because the front porch is attached to the face of the house, it provides the ornament for the front door, and as such, signals the wealth status and social position of the inhabitants. For example, the long porches of the Arts and Crafts bungalows were associated with financial misfortune during the depression (often called poverty porches) because the men who were laid off and out of work would hang out on the porch all day. Also, porches that were exposed underneath (meaning that someone could access the ground underneath the porch) were risking their fortunes. Use lattice or wooden planks to close off any access to the ground underneath the porch. Keep the porch freshly painted or varnished and remove any sign of neglect (cobwebs in the corners, etc.). Make certain that your porch does not look dormant during winter months.

Color is a simple way to welcome visitors. This cheery yellow porch invites guests to relax and enjoy the moment.

Back porches/decks. A large back porch or deck is especially important for men, as it provides a transition space between the house and the outside world where they can feel connected to the goings-on inside the house without actually being inside. Women use the back porch or deck to access the wilder, less public aspects of their psyches. If the back deck is exposed to neighbors in the rear, both men and women will feel vulnerable.

A protective lattice creates a private sanctuary out of an otherwise exposed deck.

The meandering path

Paths do much more than direct guests to your front door. Paths create mystery and wonder. As they curve out of sight or lead up to a gate, they suggest that there is more, much more, to be discovered.

A path is a journey. The paths you create influence what type of journey yours will be. Will it be fast or slow? Will the purpose of the journey be reaching the end or walking the path? In evaluating your property's paths, consider the following features:

- materials,
- relationship to nature,
- destination.

Materials. Grass, dirt, wood, brick, flagstone, rock, cement. This materials list is organized beginning with the most yin materials and ending with the most yang. The more yang your materials are, the more the emphasis shifts to control over the natural.

Relationship to nature. How you place your materials also influences how yin or yang it is. The path itself is the yang element, representing the human influence over nature. The surrounding environment or space between path elements is nature's yin influence. Stones placed close together would create a hard yang path, but the same stones placed far enough apart to allow for the grass to grow up between them is much more yin. Too much yin nature can overwhelm the yang human element, however, creating blocks on one's journey.

The grass between the stones on this path subdues the human element and increases yin.

Destination. When destinations are clearly visible from the path, the focus becomes the destination, rather than the journey. Increase the sense of mystery in your life by arranging for surprises that unfold at the end of a path, such as this seating arrangement. If the size of your yard does not allow for such surprises, delight yourself along the way by adding other whimsies such as flowering moss between stones or a unique collection of stones.

Place something at the end of your path to strengthen a sense of arrival. This secret meeting area is well worth the journey.

This sunny seat is the perfect place to spend the morning.

When a stone bench is warmed by the sun, it becomes both support-ive and energizing.

A "sit" spot

Take nature's daily cycles into account when deciding where to place sitting areas. You will need more than one sitting area to accommodate the position of the sun at different times of day. The minimum for outdoor comfort is a shady spot for easing outside in the morning, a bright sunny spot to get warm, and a cool-down area for sunsets at the end of the day. Where you place your morning and late-afternoon rest zones will depend on the shade provided by neighboring houses and surrounding trees, but keep the following feng shui wisdom in mind as well.

Morning seating areas. These need to support your visionary side (grand vistas are good here). The beginning of the day is related to the Wood element in feng shui and is best suited for envisioning new projects, planning your daily activities, or brainstorming novel solutions to old problems. As such, you should locate your morning sitting area where you feel expansive and have a view of the sky (can you recline your seat?). The sky represents uncharted territory, the realm of discovery and unlimited potential. Use your piece of sky to think outside your normal realm.

Adding an umbrella to your table gives you more control over the elements and allows the same area to serve you during different times of day.

Full-sun seating areas. Although these areas are too intense in the middle of the day and/or middle of the summer, they provide a necessary yang influence during more yin times of the year. A fall afternoon might be too cool in the shade, but the warmth of the sun is just enough to melt aching muscles and relax the entire body. Related to the fire element, full-sun areas are about letting go of the past and being fully present in the moment. It is ideal to have a lounger chair that you can lie down on and close your eyes in order to bring your consciousness 100 percent to the physical experience of total relaxation. You will not need a plug-in for your laptop here. Letting go, not productivity, is the purpose of this space.

Late afternoon seating areas. Here is a place for ingathering everything that was scattered during the day. As such, these areas are best placed next to a pool of water where the energy of the water itself can help you draw yourself back in.

Water invites reflection and slows the physical body, preparing it for a time of rest.

If you cannot sit next to a pond or hot tub, use the power of metal to help you collect your thoughts. Metal creates dense, concentrated energy patterns that will help you pull everything together and make sense out of the whole. Metal also represents refinement and letting go of anything that is out of harmony with your essence, and help you to release anything toxic that you are holding in your energy field. When it comes to the end of the day, think small cozy spots.

This rounded gate captures a magical view of the side yard, creating a sense of wonder and discovery.

A framed view

No matter how small your yard, you can still create pleasant views. The necessary element for a view is a frame to contain it. There are many different types of frames; but the frame, more than the actual view, determines the effect.

I never saw an ugly thing in my life: for let the form of an object be what it may—light, shade, and perspective will always make it beautiful.

—John Constable

To frame your views, take your camera outside. Looking around your yard through the lens will help you locate your most inspiring views. Once you have located them, you can frame them by:

- positioning sitting areas to capture a particular view;
- trailing ivy or shaping the growth of surrounding plants;
- installing a lattice, arch, or arbor;
- placing stepping stones to lead the eye down a path;
- cutting away existing shrubbery, hedges, or trees;
- elevating your view by building a deck or raised patio.

A way with water

To the Chinese, water is money. The word abundance, which comes from the Latin word "*abundare*," literally means to overflow. Water brings the energy patterns of flow, abundance, and ease to one's life. However, putting in a pond or pool is trickier than you might think. The shape, placement, and condition of the pool all affect whether your fortunes increase or diminish. If you decide to add a water feature to your yard, keep the following feng shui tips in mind.

Choose the right shape. Water does not flow in straight lines, so a straight-sided pool will not generate the same energy patterns that a curved one will. Irregular shapes imply flexibility and movement, straight lines imply control and strength. If you swim to feel free and relax, a kidney-shaped pool will help. If you swim to feel strong and in control of your life, a rectangular-shaped pool is great for you.

Embrace the house. Position your pool or pond so that it curves toward the house, embracing it, rather than bending away from the house. The inside curve is where chi builds, the outside edge is constantly losing chi. Curve your pool in to hold your chi.

A small bamboo spout has abundant ways to comfort and soothe with water.

This kidney-shaped pool encourages fluidity and relaxation.

Ba gua map

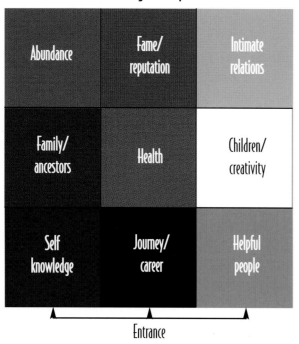

Abundance	Fame/ reputation	Intimate relations
Family/ ancestors	Health	Children/ creativity
Self knowledge	Journey/ career	Helpful people

Entrance

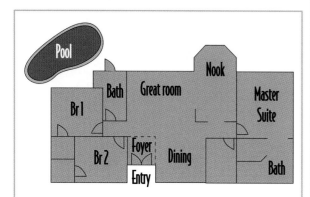

Use the pool to balance the house. If your house is missing any areas of the ba gua map, place the pool in the missing area. Because pools and ponds hold tremendous life force, this feature can bring vitality and chi to an otherwise dormant area of your yard (and your life).

Place the pool according to the ba gua. The ancient template, or map, that balances the energy that flows through a home or yard is called the ba gua. According to this map, some areas benefit from increased Water while others lose energy. The best places for a pool or pond are the front-center section of your yard (the Journey/career sector) and the rear-left section (relating to wealth and Abundance).

Stabilize a pool in the Fame area of the ba gua. Avoid placing a water feature in the Fame/reputation area of your yard (rear center). This area relates to Fire energy, which has an upward expansive dynamic, the opposite of downward-flowing water. A pond in Fame can create "damp" conditions for the heart and also dampen your reputation. If your pond or pool is already situated in the Fame area, balance the downward flow with a sprinkler head that shoots water directly up into the air and add large rocks to stabilize the volatile combination of Water and Fire.

Integrate the pool with its natural surroundings. The most interesting thing about money is that those who do not feel comfortable with it cannot seem to hold on to it. Time and again, people who acquire large sums of money quickly, lose it just as quickly. They do not know how to integrate the energy of money into their lives. It feels unnatural and alien to their personal chi and, as a result, their interaction with it is brief. Since your water feature represents your psychological ability to gather and accumulate money, you want it to appear as a natural part of your home and life. It should look as if it has been there for centuries.

Make certain the liner does not leak. Most plastic liners will leak over time and digging everything out to fix it is a monumental task. To the Chinese, leaking pools connote impending bankruptcy and financial disaster. You might want to consider the leakproof fiberglass form. These forms come in numerous shapes, depths, and sizes.

Keep the water clean. Most of us intend to put in a pond and end up with a swamp. Consider using a natural cleaning agent that will cleanse the water. Since water represents your financial situation, you do not want it murky. If you need some grime in the pond, for koi or other fish to feed from, be certain to keep a low pump running to balance the grime.

Avoid disappearing-edge pools. The illusion of water, and by association money, flowing over the edge into the abyss is not auspicious. You need to visually contain the water to hold on to the money. If you already have a disappearing edge, plant trees on the other side to create a visual boundary and strengthen the sense of containment.

Replace any fish that die. The cultural significance of dead fish in China is noteworthy. The Chinese believe that any *shar* chi (negative, intense energy) can be absorbed by the fish in a pond and that the fish willingly takes this chi in to protect its owner. If the fish dies, thank it for its generosity and assistance and replace it as soon as possible.

As beautiful as this pond is, care must be taken to clean it regularly, otherwise it will generate a stagnant energy field that will affect the owner's financial status.

40% sepia brown

25% aqua

10% oatmeal

25% coral

The curious effects of color

The colors in your home should support the way you live. This means getting the right balance between safety and stretch. Have you ever been in someone's home that you considered over-the-top, with colors so busy and intense you felt unable to relax? Likewise, I am certain you have been in homes that were too placid, unassuming, and lifeless in their color choices. You need to know your comfort range—the area between too safe on the one extreme and too intense on the other. Your comfort range is controlled by your personal need for a certain amount of safety and a certain amount of adventure in a healthy balance.

How much safety do you need?

The evocative home follows the 60/30/10 design rule. This rule means that your wall surfaces make up the largest percentage of color in a space (generally 60 percent). The flooring, rugs, window treatments, and large furniture pieces make up 30 percent, and the remaining 10 percent is in the details. That means, if you select a safe wall color, you can use risk colors in your accent items, and/or in your window treatments, furniture coverings, rugs, and decor. If, however, you have a room in which you use a risk color on the wall, such as purple or red, you need to balance out this room with other rooms in the house, so that the house overall is not more than 40 percent at risk. The more of a risker you tend to be, the closer you will be to 40 percent in risk colors; the more conservative you are, the closer you will be to 10 percent.

The 60/30/10 rule:

Wall color = 60%

Flooring & furniture = 30%

Accent pieces = 10%

Most people need between 60 percent to 90 percent safe colors and 10 percent to 40 percent risk colors. This bright red entry door will increase the adventure for the San Francisco occupants.

The drama of black adds excitement to an otherwise safe color scheme.

Which colors are safe?

While color associations vary greatly from culture to culture (See Color chart on pages 132–135), certain colors and tones are universal symbols of safety. These associations come primarily from a color's physiological effects and its representation in the natural world. For example, the color blue will not make you feel safe in a kitchen. Why? Because blue food in nature is almost always poisonous to human beings. In this case, the same blue that feels comforting and peaceful in your bedroom can actually increase anxiety and discomfort in your kitchen.

This San Francisco town house has three levels and numerous angles, requiring a color combination of primarily safe colors. Each of the following items are "safe" colors:

- ■ dark taupe accent wall,
- ■ white surrounding walls,
- ■ dark green side table.

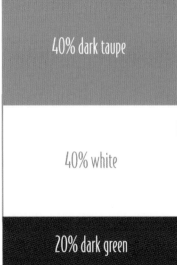

40% dark taupe

40% white

20% dark green

Reliable brown. Any brown tone—cream, beige, tan, taupe, ecru, ocher, toast, oatmeal, russet—is a safe color. Brown represents Earth energy—the enduring ground from which all nature's creations spring. Items made from brown materials tend to last over time, such as a hardwood floor or an earthen pot. Physiologically, brown carries energy lower in the body, helping a person feel more grounded and steady. Nothing creates safety and stability like brown.

Muted majesty. Adding black or brown to otherwise risky colors mutes and softens the tone. For example, red is normally a risk color. But if you add black or brown, you can produce brick red or maroon. Your body can relax and ground somewhat in a brick red or maroon room, whereas scarlet puts the body on alert. Muted colors create a stronger yin energy that will increase strength and stability in the home. Whether or not colors like terra-cotta (an orange-brown combination) or Gustavian blue (a gray-blue combination) are safety colors is often determined by the extent to which they are muted and the brightness of the surrounding colors.

Muted tones of any color help your body relax and become grounded.

Green balances the metabolic activity of the body.

116 Fair white. White connotes perfect balance and fairness. White light appears white because it reflects a balanced distribution of all the spectrum colors. If white light was not perfectly balanced in its light distribution, it would appear dingy or off-colored. White represents fairness because none of the colors are left out. A note of caution, however. White provides a high contrast background for other colors, which means that it can actually make the risky colors even brighter or "more risky" than they would be against a muted background. Because of its high-contrast nature, white makes an area more yang if combined with bright colors. To soften the yang effect, use an "aged" white that has been mixed with a muted color to soften it.

Neutral green. Like white, green also connotes balance (in between cool and warm colors) and is the color that most often represents nature and healing (the Chinese view healing as a return to balance). Physiologically, green activates the body's metabolism, balancing catabolic with anabolic processes. In a home, clear, cool, or muddy greens are better on the wall, while yellow green is more appropriate as an accent color. Just as yellow green in nature represents something that is not yet ripe, yellow green in a home represents new and rapid growth and brings in more yang chi (change and risk) than blue green, emerald green, olive green, and sage do.

White represents fairness, being a perfect balance of all the colors in the light spectrum, visible when light passes through a prism.

Gold balances yellow's warmth with brown's stability.

Gracious gold. Although yellow is a risk color, a toned-down gold version with more brown than yellow is considered safe. Gold balances yellow's warmth and sparkle with brown's stability and comfort, creating one of the most emotionally and physiologically balanced colors in the color wheel. Add a bit of green, and you have a metabolic balancer as well. The yellow in gold activates the solar plexus, which energizes an individual's personal will or strength. Healers since Egyptian times have bathed the sick in gold light to strengthen their will to live and increase their ability to fight off disease. Gold is also the color most often seen by psychics the world over as the manifestation of universal energy (not the red of Chinese lore).

Which colors are risky?

Risky colors challenge you in some way. Yang in nature, these colors generate expansion, movement, or exploration. They invite you to open, to feel more alive, and to engage with your surroundings. They accomplish this by throwing you slightly off balance. They are the unexpected, the out-of-the-ordinary, and the uniquely personal.

Lively yellow. Yellow is the most visually active color. It bounces around a room, constantly drawing and moving the eye. By itself, yellow will tire the eye faster than any other color. Yellow also activates the solar plexus in the body (relating to a person's sense of personal power). This power does not always lead to harmonious interactions, however. Research indicates that babies cry and couples argue more in a yellow room. When you add yellow to other colors, such as yellow green, the effect is always dynamic and growth-oriented. These colors are meant to move you, not settle you down for a nice cozy nap.

Yellow bounces the eye and keeps a room active.

Provocative purple. Purple is a rare color in the natural world. In foods, it signifies disintegration and rot. In animals and humans, it is the color of bruising (also a sign of a hurt or damaged system). Because of its rare appearance, purple has become associated with royalty, since only people of royal blood could afford to have purple dyes used in their clothes. Purple is excellent for opening up the body's higher energy centers and for connecting you with the more spiritual part of your being. Still, you are better off not making purple the main color of your home, but using it as an accent. An entirely purple room can lead to mental illness and the disintegration of muscular tissue.

Purple is best used as an accent. In a dominantly purple color scheme, offset with white or gold.

118

Blue slows the metabolism and lowers the heart rate. Use blue in rooms where you want to relax and let go.

Serene blue. The color of the sea and sky, blue creates feelings of peaceful serenity. It is especially appropriate in bathrooms and bedrooms, but should be avoided in kitchens (See Which colors are safe? on page 114). Although blue is an appropriate wall color for smaller rooms, not more than 40 percent of the entire home should be done in cool colors (See Your home's color balance on pages 124–126). Too many cool colors in a house affect the body's metabolism and can lead to a weakened immune system.

Outrageous orange. You do not see unripe orange food in the natural world. Pumpkins, oranges, and squashes do not turn orange until they are fully ripe. Foods typically turn orange in the fall, just as the sun's rays turn orange in the evening sky. This time of day and time of year relate to the end of the work day (or work season) and the beginning of a relaxation/celebration phase. No surprise that researchers have found that orange rooms encourage less-inhibited behavior. The social nature of orange is evidenced in the body as well. Orange stimulates the sexual organs and other bodily systems that are more social in nature (such as digestion). Thus, orange is considered the most social color.

Orange is reserved for social rooms, since it excites conversation and lowers the inhibitions.

Red is a power color, but be certain to include it only in active rooms, as it activates blood flow to the body's large muscles. Red is often best used as an accent color.

Raging red. Fight or flight is red's evolutionary response. The sight of red, which in primitive times was often caused by the sight of blood, activates blood flow to large muscles so that they can spring into action. Red drains energy from the brain and encourages instinctive primitive responses, bringing the body's fight-or-flight mechanism into play. Bright red is also used by bugs, birds, and animals to warn off predators, since evolution has taught that a nasty sting, poison, or hidden weapon can be concealed by red. Avoid red-and-white combinations since red's complementary color is green. After looking at a red wall, the white wall takes on a greenish hue, causing nausea and headaches.

Note: Pink falls into the red category. Use it only in select rooms or as an accent. Not more than 20 percent of the house should ever be pink.

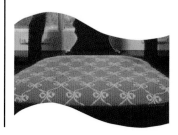

Reserved black. Black is an unusual risk color. Rather than opening and exciting a person too much, black creates withdrawal and introspection. Cool, aloof, detached, and reserved are all adjectives that indicate black's withdrawal mechanism. Because people are typically more withdrawn in formal situations, black has also become associated with formality, sophistication, and modernism (which represents detachment from tradition). This detachment gives black the ability to separate one energy pattern from another (such as a black picture frame defining where the picture ends and the wall begins). For these reasons, black should only be used to define a space, not fill it.

Black is formal, glamorous, and reserved. Be certain to balance a black wall with plenty of surrounding white or cream.

121

Safe color combinations

The following color combinations create a safe, secure environment, using a 90 percent safe to 10 percent risk ratio. Use safety combinations in rooms where you need to feel secure, comforted, and grounded.

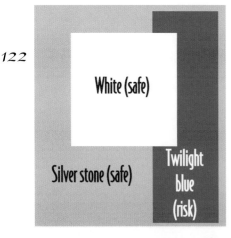

White (safe)

Silver stone (safe)

Twilight blue (risk)

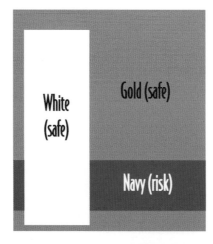

White (safe)

Gold (safe)

Navy (risk)

Golden haze (safe)

Deep gold (safe)

Pine green (risk)

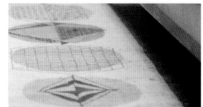

Sage green (safe)

Creamy yellow (risk)

Shell pink (risk)

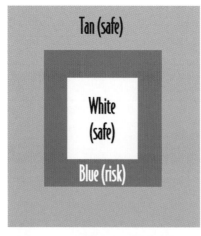

Tan (safe)

White (safe)

Blue (risk)

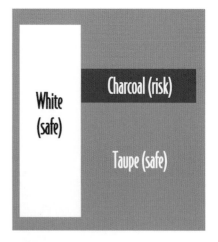

White (safe)

Charcoal (risk)

Taupe (safe)

Risk color combinations

The following color combinations invite exploration and adventure into the home with a 60 percent safe to 40 percent risk ratio. Use risk color combinations in rooms where you want to dream and imagine.

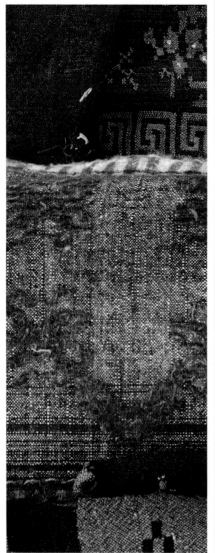

Your home's color balance

The human eye has a warm color bias. Humans need an overall balance of 60 percent to 75 percent warm colors, to 25 percent to 40 percent cool colors in indoor environments. Balancing cool and warm colors has more to do with the physical properties of the eye and how we perceive color than it does with personal preference. The human eye can distinguish four different colors through the cones: red, green, blue, and yellow (not the "three" primary colors you learned in school). The eye can also pick up a variance in luminosity (light to dark). With these six variables (four colors added to light and dark), humans see thousands of color variations.

The eye has adapted genetically. There is a much greater percentage of "warm color" cones in human eyes (cones that see red, yellow, and green) than the percentage of "cool color" cones (cones that see blue). This genetic fact results in strange psychological implications. If your home is decorated with too many cool colors, the cones will not fire as much as they would if you had more warm colors. When the cones do not fire, the light message does not get passed from the cones to the neurons. And what the neurons do not register cannot get transmitted to the brain. The result is similar to staying in a dimly lit interior and not going out in the sun. Over time, you are bound to feel fatigued, depressed, and run down.

Figuring your home's color balance. To figure out what percentage of your home has cool colors and what percentage is warm, use the 60/30/10 rule. If you have rooms that are not on the Color balance chart at right, add a row for each additional room. Once you have determined where your home falls within the warm/cool color range, add or subtract as necessary to bring it within optimal range.

Using the chart. For wall color, mark the 60 percent row. For window treatments, flooring and furniture, mark the 30 percent row. For accent objects and decor pieces, mark the 10 percent row. Add the percentages for both warm and cool and divide by the number of rooms.

Color balance chart

	Warm %			Cool %		
	Walls 60%	Furniture & floor 30%	Accents 10%	Walls 60%	Furniture & floor 30%	Accents 10%
Living room						
Dining room						
Kitchen						
Great room						
Family room						
Bathroom 1						
Bathroom 2						
Entry						
Mud room						
Work space (office, den)						
Loft/play area						
Bedroom 1						
Bedroom 2						
Bedroom 3						
Closets (storage area)						
Hallways						
Subtotals in %						

	Sum of 2 columns	Total # of Rms	Home's Color %
Warm subtotal		÷	=
Cool subtotal	÷		=

Use your body as your guide. So what percentage is optimal for you? Are you a 60/40 percent person or a 75/25 percent person? I suggest you use your body as your guide. If you are storing too much energy (bloating, extra weight, or emotional heaviness), increase the amount of warm colors in the home. If you are attracting more energy than you can handle (feeling flushed, hyper, anxious, or stressed), increase the amount of cool colors.

126

The gold and white safe colors on the walls are offset by the red and green.

Balancing with color

Paint can bring balance to your rooms in some fun ways. Varying colors and even shades of the same color can change your visual perception, allowing you to create some dynamic effects.

The long narrow room. Some living rooms or family rooms feel like a long narrow bowling hall. Paint color can help you here. If you paint the short end-walls one shade lighter than the long sidewalls, the short end-walls will seem larger. This is because light colors visually expand an area (make it more yang) and darker colors contract (make it more yin).

This room uses color to give more visual weight to the end-wall, reducing the emphasis on the long narrow sidewalls.

The dark wall color helps contain the chi in this wall of windows.

The square boxy room. If your room is too boxy, painting one wall an accent color will shift the feel of the room to a rectangular shape. A brighter or darker color is best because the color will draw the eye and shift the focal point of the room to one end.

The wall of windows. A darker paint color can help you balance out a wall of windows. The natural light coming through your windows will instantly "fade" your wall color. The window wall will look washed out and paler than the remaining walls. Painting this wall one shade darker will help it match the rest of the room better and enable you to keep more chi force from going out the windows.

Naming color

I used to refer to "muted" tones as "muddy" tones, and then wondered why clients did not want to paint their house a "muddy" color. How you refer to the colors you select impacts your emotional body because the name of the color holds an emotional charge.

You can use this naming effect to your advantage by selecting a name for your wall color that embodies the characteristics and emotional energy you want the color to bring into the home. Consider the different impact of selecting "sharkskin gray" over "evening sky." They could both be a bluish gray color, but the name itself makes the one feel aggressive and masculine and the other feel peaceful and serene. (I will let you figure out which one is which.)

Set against a backdrop of neutral white, this mountain painting draws the eye away from the sharp edge of the wall.

The nine-drop ritual

The following ritual is a wonderful way to bring the energy of a certain color into a room without actually painting the entire room that color. If you are familiar with the colors associated with each area of the ba gua, you might wonder how all this color information is going to fit into those nine ba gua sectors. Do not worry, you do not have to paint your dining room purple just because it falls in the Abundance area of your home, and Intimate Relations areas do not need to be pink. The nine-drop ritual is a method of using intention to energetically charge your paint with the vibration of that ba gua sector's associated color.

Ba gua map

Abundance	Fame/ reputation	Intimate relations
Family/ ancestors	Health	Children/ creativity
Self knowledge	Journey/ career	Helpful people

Entrance

Purchase nine sampler tubes of paint, one for each area of the ba gua. (If you are using latex or acrylic paint, you can usually get samplers from the craft store, rather than having to buy pints from the paint store.) You will need: black, blue, green, purple, red, pink, yellow, white, and gray.

Perform the following with each ba gua area. Place nine drops of the color associated with that ba gua area (such as black for the Journey/career area) into each gallon of the paint you will be using in that part of the house. Using a stir stick, stir clockwise and repeat the following phrase, "I ask that the vibration of these nine drops energize and transform the vibration in this gallon of paint, so that the entire gallon will hold the energetic pattern represented by these drops. I ask that any natural forces present in my home who are willing to assist with this process do so now." Stir at least nine times, making certain the drops are completely mixed in.

You will not see a color change after performing this ritual, but you will feel a difference once the paint gets on the wall.

Making color flow

Second only to light, color carries energy through the home, linking one room to the next, affecting your emotions, balance, and overall mood. Just as important as the colors you select are the way in which you combine those colors into an overall house scheme.

When every room is the same color. The most common approach to handling color flow is to paint every room in the house the same color. This approach guarantees that the energy of one room will flow into the next and that the eye will not be greeted with harsh transitions as you move from place to place. This approach is fine as long as you select a safety color as your wall color and vary the 30/10 colors in each room. A house in which everything is cream-colored, including cream walls, cream carpet, and cream-colored furniture would be quite difficult to live in because it creates too much of the same energy pattern.

You can introduce a color into a room by simply adding a candle as an accent.

Honey-colored hardwood floors and rich wood accents warm the white walls throughout the home. The blue in this room sets it apart from neighboring areas.

By tying the color scheme into the brick wall and the green plants, the paint colors themselves feel more organic. The overall vibration of the home rises whenever you bring greater harmony to a combination of parts by drawing them together in a way that allows each part to share its energy with the other parts of the home.

The hallway picks up the terra-cotta accent color of the kitchen and living room as its primary color. The gold retreats and becomes the background color.

When each room is a different color. For "wild and crazy" artists, this approach seems ideal, and it can be equally wonderful. Balance is the key to making it work. What feels balanced to you will depend on how much safety and how much risk you need.

Decide on three to four colors. For your color theme, these colors need to play well together. Use both safety and risk colors in your combination to make certain it will serve your energetic and physical body, as well as your design sense. Three-color schemes are suitable for smaller homes. Once you move into more than four rooms, you will need four colors to create enough variety in your combinations. (See Safe color combinations on page 122 and Risk color combinations on page 123 for help selecting balanced color schemes.)

Plug the colors in your scheme into different parts of the 60/30/10 rule. Use this method in different rooms. By changing the percentage of each color in various rooms, you can achieve variety while maintaining flow throughout the home overall. For example, you might use burgundy on your living-room walls, on the tablecloth in the dining room, and on the rug in your hallway.

Select a unifying color that will show up in every room in the same way. For example, visually unite your rooms by painting the trim white in each room, using hardwood floors in each room, or selecting chrome fixtures in each room.

The gold walls are the primary color in this room. The green couch and plants are supporting accents.

Color chart

Color is more than the sum of its meanings. That said, the chart below (each color's qualities are listed in order of lowest to highest consciousness) can help you scan for colors whose meanings will suit and support the intended energy of a specific room or project.

	Physical effects	Cultural associations	Emotional impact	Psychological attributes
Red	Increases heart rate, increases blood pressure and blood flow, increases adrenaline, drains blood from the brain and redirects it to large muscle groups (acting without thinking)	**China:** Energy, good luck **USA:** Courage, passion **India:** Marriage **Native American:** Faith, communication **Universal:** Nature's sex stimulus, as in red lips	Angry, outraged, irritable, passionate, courageous 	**Red:** Domination, survival, confrontation, aggression, self-absorption, good luck, audacity, activity, courage **Maroon:** Self-sacrifice (combines red's courage with black's association with death) **Magenta:** Innovation (combines red's audacity with purple's insightfulness)
Pink	Balances the effects of red with those of white 	**USA:** Physical weakness **China:** Marriage **Native American:** Creativity, working **Universal:** Romantic love	Weepy, needy, friendly, tender, compassionate 	Instability, immaturity, femininity, softness, sensitivity, faithfulness, self-love
Orange	Balances the hormones; stimulates sexual organs; aids with infertility; governs the intestines, lower abdominals, adrenals, and kidneys; helps body recover from shock	**USA:** Clowns and false attempts at cheerfulness, obesity **Tibet:** Eternal life **Native American:** Kinship, learning **Universal:** Fruit and fruitfulness	Desirous, encouraging, cheerful, happy, concerned for others' well-being, content	Deceitful, overpowering, hyperactivity, stimulation, attraction, success, playfulness, sociability, joyful

Physical effects	Cultural associations	Emotional impact	Psychological attributes

Yellow

Physical effects	Cultural associations	Emotional impact	Psychological attributes
Stimulates the liver, pancreas, solar plexus, spleen, and middle stomach; affects the nervous system; stimulates the flow of gastric juices (which helps release fears, phobias, and physical toxins); stimulates lymphatic system (which relieves menstrual difficulties)	**Tibetan:** Buddhist monk robes **Pagan cultures:** Sun worship **Europe:** Lower classes **USA:** Federal yellow, colonial times **Native American:** Love, overcoming challenges **Universal:** Sunshine, energy source, commonality	Mean, anxious, sassy, egocentric, optimistic, confident, cheerful, happy 	**Yellow:** Treachery, manipulation, craftiness, verbal expression, charm, mental acuteness, accelerated memory, confidence, strength, intelligence, personal power **Green-yellow:** Cowardice **Gold:** Affluence, persuasion, attraction of cosmic influences

Green

Physical effects	Cultural associations	Emotional impact	Psychological attributes
Increases heart rate, increases blood pressure and blood flow, increases adrenaline, drains blood from the brain and redirects it to large muscle groups (acting without thinking) 	**Egyptian myths:** Osiris, god of death; ironically meant hope/spring **Celtic myths:** Green man, god of fertility **Greek myths:** Olive green, the symbol for peace **Roman myths:** Venus, goddess of love attracted to emerald green **Middle ages:** Fertility symbol **USA:** Money, finances, employment **Native American:** Living willfully **Asian:** Prosperity, luck, eternity **Universal:** Nature, growth, health, freshness	Betrayed, envious, jealous, greedy, trapped, ambitious, united with someone or a cause, loving	**Green:** Indecisive, easygoing, family focus, longevity, health, balance, harmony **Dark green:** Ambition, greed, financial prosperity, long-term success 

	Physical effects	Cultural associations	Emotional impact	Psychological attributes
Blue				
	Affects the throat, thyroid gland, and the base of the skull; slows the respiratory system; lowers blood pressure; stabilizes erratic heart rate **Indigo blue:** Affects sinus glands, eyes, and pineal gland	**Roman empire:** Public servant uniforms **USA:** Police and other public servants, solitude **Native American:** Intuition **Universal:** Loyalty, honesty	Depressed, withdrawn, lonely, sad, peaceful, understanding, tranquil, forgiving 	Depression, sadness, truthfulness, loyalty, wisdom **Light blue:** Patience **Dark blue:** Impulsivity 
Purple				
	Stimulates the top of the head including brain activity, scalp, crown, and pineal gland	**Europe:** Royalty **USA:** Luxury, gay (lavender) **Native American:** Wisdom, gratitude, spiritual healing **Universal:** Nature's symbol for poison, rarity, spiritual	Suicidal, depressed, calm, in tune, ethereal, enlightened 	**Purple:** Obsession, tension, ambition, progression, psychic ability, power, spirituality, wisdom **Lavender:** Mental illness, intuition, dignity
White				
	Absorbs none of the color rays, bouncing all the colors back to the eye; cleanses imbalances from the entire body	**Asian:** Mourning (they wear white to funerals to keep spirits from invading their aura), children **USA:** Sterile, neutral **Native American:** Magnetism, sharing **Universal:** Purity, cleanliness, innocence, balance,	Cold, distant, disconnected, sarcastic, peaceful, sincere, 	Sterility, sarcasm, sharpness, balance, inclusivity, fairness, exactness, precision, spirituality

134

Physical effects	Cultural associations	Emotional impact	Psychological attributes

Black

Black absorbs all the color rays, reflecting nothing back to the eye; slows all bodily processes (which can help with hyperactivity); draws energy inward; promotes retention of fluids	**Europe:** Black priest robes signify submission to God **Native American:** Hearing from within, harmony, listening **Asian:** Water energy, feminine energy **USA:** Formal, modernism, the unconscious, protection **Universal:** Formality, death, absorption	Suicidal, depressed, negative, heavy, confused, insecure, vengeful, protected, safe, still, serene 	Evil, villainous, draining, discord, submission, modern, formal, sophisticated, prudent, authoritative, powerful 

Gray

Considered the result of a physiological breakdown or disintegration of bodily tissue	**Asian:** Community, travel, spirit entities **Native American:** Honor, friendship **Universal:** Spoiled food	Apathetic, passive, uncommunicative, neutral, calm	**Gray:** Collapse, disease, decay, confusion, self-reliance, self-sufficiency, mediation, complexity, neutrality **Silver:** Dreaming, astral connection, stability

Brown

Brings energy into the lower half of the body, slows metabolism, increases catabolic activity (which builds up muscles, tissues, and other growths)	**Japan:** Neutrality, connection with nature **USA:** Material increase, telepathy, associated with animals **Native American:** Knowing, self-discipline **Universal:** Solid, stable, mature, earthy	Indecisive, hesitant, stuck, comfortable, grounded, calm 	Barren, restrictive, masculinity, being comfortable, studiousness, reliability, genuineness 

This magical place evokes the energies of many shapes, bringing them all into perfect balance. The branching triangle of the bougainvillea, the pillar in the upward-rising fireplace, the rectangular tile inset, and the curved arch in the twig chair all rest on a grounded foundation of brick squares.

I believe that good design is magical and not to be lightly tinkered with. The difference between a great design and a lousy one is in the meshing of the thousand details.
— Ted Nelson

Feng shui shapes

The shape of an object directs every energy force that interacts with it. How shapes move energy has been studied for thousands of years, with Egyptian, Hebrew, Greek, Roman, Native American, and Hindu cultures, all contributing their puzzle piece. This study forms the center of our space program and allows airplanes to fly and aerodynamic cars to drive faster. Even in your living room—cupping a round wooden bowl or flattening your hand along the top of a table—shape alters your experience.

The center and the edge

Every shape must have a center, a pivot point. In feng shui, the point is the place at which potential energy becomes manifest in form. From a single point, energy issues forth from the realm of the infinitely possible—pure potential—into the world of form and limitation. Hence, the creation of any object begins with movement from a beginning point outward until it reaches an edge. The edge is as important as the center. It is the edge that directs the energy of the object back toward the center, keeping the energy moving perpetually from center to edge and back to center. How the energy of an object moves from its center to its edge determines its impact on other objects.

A simple circle of grass can activate an otherwise dormant outdoor space. By defining a clear center, the circle also shapes the edge, pulling the furniture into an active and lively conversation area.

The three objects were placed on this table to bring the focusing energy of the triangle into the home's living area.

The year is a circle around the world.
—Dakota Tribe

Primary shapes

The triangle. Triangles are a means of moving energy quickly and focusing it toward a specific point. The chi gathers at the base and is directed out of the point at the top, much like narrowing the nozzle on your garden hose. The spray of water becomes considerably more intense and penetrating the more you narrow the stream. This means that the chi moving out of the top of a triangle is usually not harmonious or helpful for human beings, and they should avoid positioning themselves at the end of the point. Triangles should be used to direct chi to a desired location other than sitting or work areas. Triangles also represent merging heavenly forces with those of humankind and Mother Earth. Viewed historically as the three primary forces in the universe, triangles remind us to look at the spiritual (heaven), physical (earth), and mental (human) implications of any decision.

The square. Squares are nature's way of holding on to an energy pattern in order to slow change and stabilize a process. The four corners of the square form the foundational building block for most structures and even out the distribution of energy from the center equally on all four sides. All this steadiness is great; however, a house full of nothing but squares and rectangles might be too anchored and become rigid or inflexible. If family members tend to defend their positions staunchly, even when they have good reason to change their minds, you might want to exchange some of those squares for other shapes.

The sphere. Spheres represent wholeness, completion, and perfection. The entire energetic journey is captured in the sphere, from its beginning point to its fullest extension and its condensation back into a pinpoint at the center. Spherical elements remind the body of this constantly cycling energy pattern and encourage constant growth and evolution. Relating to community and helpful people, circles and spheres are about working together, rather than squaring off in separate corners. Anything round will keep chi moving, though, and nothing settles for long around a circular table or work space.

Kidney shapes. Irregular or kidney shapes are considered Water energy patterns, a representation of the Tao. They move energy out from the center in a slow, meandering current. The more curved the sides are, the longer it takes the chi to travel around the edges before coming back to center. To use kidney shapes in your home is to symbolize that you are in the flow and that all good things will come to you exactly when you need them.

The pillar. Reaching up into the sky, the pillar has the ability to extend your energy into places you have never been before. Related to Wood energy, pillars represent strength, perseverance, determination, and fortitude. Historically, pillars have been symbols of humans' ability to both connect and communicate with the divine. Temple pillars, poles, spires, even Jacob's ladder, are all vertical columns that direct the energy of the earth plane up into the heavens. Referred to as the *Axis Mundi*, this vertical vortex between heaven and earth was considered to be the source through which the heavens energized and supported the earth. Pillars also represent the human element in the heaven, earth, man triangle, because the human element stands upright on the earth and interfaces with heaven on the behalf of earth. The pillar is a strong way to help family members feel reconnected to something more than themselves and want to stand up and take action.

A pillar suggests a link between the yang energies of heaven and the yin forces of the earth.

This colorful stack of Shaker boxes creates its own *Axis Mundi* for this area, directing the chi straight up.

This artful application of the sun's rising rays forms an arch over this otherwise square fireplace, pushing the chi upward and helping to lift the oppressive chi from the ceiling beams.

The arch. Ancient temples are filled with arches. The pillars of the temples rise up, supporting the arch because it symbolized the bridge to heaven. Arches today represent the influence of the divine on earth. Sunrises, sunsets, and rainbows all form an arch across the sky, bringing in heaven's yang chi in the morning and taking it away again at the end of the day. In China, the arch is related to the Metal element, the energy pattern of the Helpful People ba gua area. Use archways to symbolize a passageway to an out-of-the-ordinary place or connection with your own spiritual being.

The cross. The cross represents the vertical pillar energy of heaven or spirit and its interface with the horizontal earthly realm. Stemming from Creation myths, like the following, the cross has been around long before its current association with Christianity. The Absolute "divided itself into heaven and earth, thereby creating the *Axis Mundi*—the pole situated at the center of the world, holding up the canopy of heaven and connecting it with the earth. It thus became the central axis connecting and penetrating the horizontal states of being by passing through their centers." (R. Guenon, *Symbolism of the Cross*)

This living-room arrangement creates a perfect cross with the couch and chair on the horizontal axis and the ottoman and chair on the vertical axis.

- What time does my body usually want to wake up without an alarm? (the wake-up zone)

- When do I feel the most productive? (the work zone)

- When do I want to be around other people? (the social zone)

- When am I most likely to relax? (the relaxation zone)

- When do my creative juices start flowing? (the creativity zone)

- I sleep best between the hours of _____ and _____. (renewal zone)

Feng shui zones

The zone approach to feng shui is a method of taking into account how your personal biological clock and tendencies interface with the natural rhythms of the sun's 24-hour cycle. Individuals respond differently to the sun's signals of when to sleep and when to rise. Design books tend to assume that everyone rises with the sun, is active until about 3:00 or 4:00 P.M., slows down in the evening, goes to sleep at 10:00 P.M., and sleeps through the night. If that were true, however, sleep agents would not be the third most commonly sold over-the-counter drug. Have you ever met someone who did not wake up until 11:00 A.M., got going around 4:00 P.M., and was fully functional around 9:00 P.M.? Do not you think this person would want to set his house up differently than someone who got up with the sun and was in bed by 9:00 P.M.? To understand your personal timing, answer the questions in the outside column on this page and fill in the Time-zone wheel, then read the definitions of each zone on page 143. After that, you will be ready to make some adjustments to where things are located, based on how your clock is ticking.

Time-zone wheel

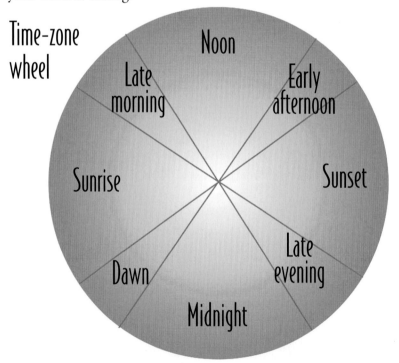

When your cycle is out of sync

The Time-zone wheel on page 142 will help you understand whether or not your personal time zones are out of sync with the sun's. If they are, you will need to use your environment to help you create the kind of energy for each zone that the sun normally creates during that time of the day.

6:00 A.M.–12:00 NOON (Wood to Fire)

This phase is related to the wake-up zone and the work zone. During this phase, Wood energy takes root in the yin earth and uses the energy patterns of expansion, movement, and change to slowly increase yang. If you sleep until noon, you have missed the sun's increasingly yang acceleration and must provide that momentum for yourself. Waking up at a different time can leave you feeling tired all day long.

12:00 NOON–6:00 P.M. (Fire to Earth)

Yang reaches its zenith during this stage, the transformational time of Fire. This Fire phase is related to the social zone. If you are not particularly social in the middle of the day, you will need something other than the sun to melt your boundaries and intensify your connections. After about 3:00 P.M., the yang begins to wither, slowly decreasing. As it decreases, it moves into an Earth phase again, the transitional element between yin and yang. If you never got revved up in the first place, this gradually sinking chi will leave you flat and lacking energy. Because this is an Earth time (around 4:00 P.M.), you will be tempted to reach for snacks of an Earth nature, including sweets, carbohydrates, and starches. This will further deplete your yang.

6:00 P.M.–12:00 MIDNIGHT (Earth to Metal)

Earth's density leads to Metal's contraction, allowing the earth's energy to be drawn back into a central core. This is a time of increasing yin. This phase relates to the relaxation zone and the creativity zone. Although the nature of creativity and relaxation depends upon the individual's primary element (a Fire person needs different things to relax than a Metal person), in general, this time of day is pulling inward, contracting, and refining. The sun sinks, the temperature cools off, and the earth's chi gradually becomes more yin. If you go to sleep before midnight, you can take advantage of the earth's increasing yin, which allows you to reach a deeper state of relaxation. If you do not go to sleep until after midnight, you are fighting the entire planet's momentum, as the next phase begins a gradual return to yang.

12:00 MIDNIGHT–6:00 A.M. (Metal to Water)

Metal's contraction brings the chi to a still point deep within. This deep stillness is Water's time to replenish chi reservoirs and restore tissues. Rising too much before 6:00 A.M. short-circuits the body's restoration process and can weaken the immune system. If your renewal zone does not fall between midnight and 6:00 A.M., you reduce the body's ability to hold Water chi, making deep restful sleep more and more of a novelty. (This applies even if you wake up during this time and then go back to sleep.)

The wake-up zone

This zone is an area in your home where you prepare to meet your day. The purpose of this space is to ease you into your day so that the transition from being asleep (yin) to forging ahead with full steam (yang) is made with grace and gentleness. Oftentimes, this area is your bed, a bathroom, or a breakfast nook. The function of this space is a limbo land—a place where nothing is expected from you and you can gather whatever forces you need to move into a more active phase.

Looking at your Time-zone wheel, pinpoint when you wake up. The traditional time associated with this zone is early in the morning, between 6:00 A.M. and 9:00 A.M. If your wake-up time differs, adjust for that difference by creating a place of transition in your home.

144

Your wake-up zone should help you transition from a state of complete relaxation to a state of intense activity.

The transition from Water to Wood. This transition is the most trying on the body and needs to happen gradually. Use Earth energy to support yourself while moving from a Water state of deep sleep to a Wood state of full activity. Earth energy is about holding chi, not moving it. You need a place that will physically hold you, such as your bed, a bathtub, or a deep comfy chair.

The lighting should be dimmed and localized. Try to avoid bright or diffused lighting. Just as your muscles are warming up, your eyes need a gradual transition as well.

Place your wake-up zone near a heat outlet or sunny window. During this state, your body has digested everything you ate the day before and is at its lowest biological temperature. If the sun is already up and streaming through a window when you wake up, great. If not, make certain that your wake-up zone is near a heat vent or that there is a blanket nearby.

Keep surfaces soft. A couch or pillowed nook works better for this zone than hard blunt surfaces. After a sleep cycle, your aura is more vulnerable than at other times of the day and you will be more affected by sharp surfaces.

Give yourself a chunk of time. Allow yourself five minutes to an hour in which you require absolutely nothing of yourself. Your ability to sleep deeply and relax will be greatly enhanced if your body knows it has a period of non-doing when it first wakes up.

Do not mix your wake-up zone and work zone. If you select a space for your wake-up zone that also holds reminders of all the things you need to get done that day, you will be tempted to give up this invaluable time in order to move on to something more "productive." This is why you should not put your office in your bedroom.

Adding pillows to this metal daybed softens it and increases its ability to support the owner's vulnerability.

The work zone

Your work zone should motivate and inspire you to action. Whether it is an office, a kitchen, or a garden, this area is where your productive action-oriented self gets to shine. This zone is not about relaxing, taking it easy, or socializing. It is about manifesting in the physical realm whatever ideas, thoughts, or desires were generated during the relaxation and renewal stages.

Inspire yourself. A work zone needs avenues of inspiration. The link between the fantasy world and reality, a work zone needs links to the realm of imagination and spirit so that you do not lose sight entirely of why you are doing all this work in the first place. By adding a small fountain, a picture of a stream, or some other Water symbol, you can keep your Wood nourished and your projects flourishing.

Gather your tools together. Identify the tools of your trade and do your best to gather them all together into one workspace. Do you need a computer, kitchen sink, art supplies, internet connection, or stereo to do your work? If so, how many different rooms in your house do you need to access in order to have access to all your supplies? Reorganize cupboards, drawers, or countertops so that your work supplies are in one place. From this desk the owner can access:

- phone and phone message pad,
- computer,
- schedule and day planner,
- office supplies,
- fax machine,
- garbage (underneath),
- filing drawers.

The social zone

The social zone recognizes that we are all interdependent and participating in numerous communities at any given time. Just as we need places to be alone, we need places that facilitate coming together. How and when we choose to be together in community varies considerably. Looking at your Time-zone wheel, identify your best social hours. The earth's Fire phase is between 12:00 NOON and 3:00 P.M. If that is your time and you are normally at work then, make certain your workplace has enjoyable coworkers or that you take the time to go out to lunch with your friends. If you are an evening socializer, modern society is set up to help you, since most social interactions occur in the evening after the workday. If you like company first thing in the morning, consider an early-morning walking partner or join a morning rowing club. If you tend to socialize after most people have gone to bed, your social space will need elements (such as a built-in bar or large-screen TV) that support nocturnal activities.

A cold passageway was transformed into a delightful sun room off the kitchen. Adding this room gave the owner a casual social zone in addition to the more formal living room.

Anything that captivates and delights the senses increases the sociability of a space.

The social zone is a Fire area. Fire energy represents the ability to let go of boundaries and inhibitions, connecting with others in an intimate, open way. Fire energy is stimulated by the senses. Therefore, the more senses you can activate in your social area, the easier it will be for people to open up there. Do you have a sound system? Is there food or drink available? Are the furnishings tactile? Does it smell good? Can you see beautiful, interesting, or stimulating things? Are there living things, such as animals or flowers in full bloom? Anything that activates the senses will enhance this area.

Curve your furniture to bring your guests together. Seating areas turned slightly toward each other, but not directly facing each other, allow guests to relax. Seats directly facing each other without furniture in between (such as an ottoman or coffee table) tend to feel confrontational and confining, rather than inviting.

150 **Use lighting to set the mood.** Increase intimacy in social settings by lowering the lights. The brighter the lights, the more exposed and vulnerable people feel, especially when getting to know a stranger. Lamplighting is especially helpful, because people gravitate toward pools of light. A few well-placed lamps can draw in even those individuals who tend to hang out on the periphery of social events.

The curved shape of this couch helps guests open up and converse with each other.

The relaxation zone

A time for relaxation can occur at any time during the daily cycle, from first thing in the morning to late at night. More than time of day, the five elements are more helpful in understanding what a person needs from the environment to "let it all go." For example, a Fire-energy person needs Fire energy in order to relax, which may take the form of alcohol or other stimulants. A Metal-energy person can only relax after cleaning up and getting everything ready for the next day. If you do not know your primary element, read through each of the following paragraphs and see which one describes you most, then set up your relaxation zone accordingly.

Nothing is more relaxing than water. Even a picture of a stream, the ocean shore, or a waterfall can induce relaxation.

This daybed works during the day when sunlight is streaming in through the window. If you tend to relax at night, however, when the window is dark and the metal frame is cool, this spot is not for you.

152 **How Metal energy relaxes.** If you tend to relax in the evening, you might be a Metal-energy type. Since Metal constricts and pulls energy in, it might seem strange to think that Metal energy can help you relax. However, constricting energy is only part of Metal's role. Metal is also the sorting, distilling pattern that allows you to organize, make sense of, and place into meaningful categories, all the various events of the day. Without Metal's tendency to analyze, you would not know which parts of the day were the most meaningful to you or on which interactions you wanted to follow up. To help Metal relax, place cleaning supplies or organizing tools (such as list-making or planner entries) in your relaxation zone. For you, a few minutes of evening organizing or cleaning can clear the way for a deeper state of relaxation.

Arranging items on her bulletin board is a favorite relaxer for this Metal-energy client.

How Earth energy relaxes. If late afternoon to early evening is your time of day to let go, you might be an Earth-energy type. An Earth-energy person needs grounding in order to function. This means that Earth cannot relax until it first establishes a strong enough grounding that the person can let go of the many energies that build up in the aura like static cling on clothing. If you have a lot of Earth energy, your grounding cord is your way of letting go of anything that no longer serves you. Your form of grounding might be walking the dog, watering the grass, gardening, cooking, reading the newspaper, or swinging on a porch bench. Identify what activities help you ground and place the items needed for those activities in your home's relaxation zone. For example, hanging your dog's leash or your gardening gloves where you will see them every day will increase your grounding and support your need to relax.

A hammock or porch swing is a great way to relax. With your feet up off the floor, you will not be as tempted to jump up and attend to things as you would otherwise.

How Water energy relaxes. Can you only let go late at night when everyone else is in bed? Water energy might be your guiding force. Using the force of gravity, Water's flowing energy gradually slows and sinks until it reaches a point of absolute stillness. It is in this deep still place that Water finds the spiritual connection and resonance it needs to make sense out of the day's events. Once connected to the inner realm, external events become understandable and tolerable. Without this internal connection, it becomes increasingly difficult for a Water-energy person to relax. Rushing water is not the key here, rather slow-flowing chi and stillness will serve you better. Therefore, select a small fountain, a journal, or a meditation cushion to find your way inward, and make certain your relaxation zone has dark, not light, colors.

A quiet corner to sit in is usually all that Water requires to relax.

How Fire energy relaxes. Associated with the heat of noonday and the intensity of summer, Fire energy requires constant stimulation. Because of this need, Fire-energy people tend to be easily addicted, turning to smoking, alcohol, shopping, or sensual pleasures to raise the Fire in their bodies to a high enough level that they can "relax." Fire craves the experience of transcendence, escaping the limitations of self and merging with another person's energy field. To fulfill this need, Fire-energy types are often "touchy" people, giving others a hug or a brush on the arm, because contact reassures them and helps them feel safe. To experience the mundane or the ordinary feels like a trap that could snuff out their very life force. The key for Fire is to find ways to experience the beautiful, the extraordinary, and the sensational within the mundane ordinary world in which we all live. To be caught up and transfixed in a beautiful play of rain against your window or the smell of lavender on your sheets can satisfy Fire's passion without excess or destruction. Your relaxation zone needs sensual stimuli and connection with others (such as a cozy place to snuggle on the couch). Only then will you feel safe enough to truly relax.

154

Beauty has the power to seduce Fire into a relaxed state.

How Wood energy relaxes. Seem to keep going all day long? You are probably a Wood-energy type. Relaxed Wood energy might seem like an oxymoron, since Wood is the energy related to action and movement, but even Wood needs to relax. Most Wood-energy people continue to go until they drop, using utter fatigue or sickness to help them relax. If you want to be able to relax without getting sick, you need to coax your Wood into slowing down before it reaches exhaustion. Here is how:

- Allow for brief pauses, time-outs, in which you utterly let go of whatever project you are working on.
- Ten-minute power naps are a favorite Wood-energy break, as are stretches you can do at your desk.
- Try standing up and touching your toes between phone calls or giving yourself a neck or finger massage.
- Another Wood relaxant is learning how to do just one thing at a time.

Since Wood is accustomed to juggling five things at once, slowing down enough to do just one thing, such as drive the car (without picking up the cell phone, eating lunch, or jotting down notes), is a huge move forward in the relaxation department. Identify one place in which you commit yourself to do only one thing at a time. This area will function as your relaxation zone.

The creative zone

Want a place in your home that jump-starts your creative energy and gets your juices flowing? Like the relaxation zone, the creative zone is determined primarily by the elemental typing of the person. Often associated with the Metal element (just one type of creative expression), creativity means connecting with what the Taoists call the "Tao" or "Source." It is the life-force energy that runs through us and encompasses us at all times. By connecting with that life force, we can better understand how our gifts express and give shape to that force. Creativity is our expression of Source that stems from our unique experience of it. To understand what type of space might inspire your creative offerings, read on.

Earth energy gets creative. The primal mother figure, Earth expresses life force by nurturing and caretaking others. Earth energy is most creative when coming up with ways to care for and support others. You know your Earth energy is at work when you find yourself doing things for others that you would not do for yourself, such as making your neighbors a nice dinner or sewing elaborate Halloween costumes for your children. Your creative zone might be your kitchen, your sewing room, your garage, your dinner table, or your living-room sofa. Wherever you find yourself artistically expressing the desire to care for others, you have discovered Earth's creative zone.

Making something from Mother Earth, such as this wreath, will nurture Earth energy's creative side.

Water energy gets creative. Water is the depths of our being, our still point, and our connection to realms beyond the earthly realm. Therefore, Water's creativity strives to touch the core of a person and offer a glimpse of things that lie beyond the self. Water creativity has some challenging aspects, though. For example, you cannot rush Water's deep insights or force Water to compromise its message for the sake of a director's whims or budget. Integrity, honesty, and self-sacrifice are Water's trademarks, as many a starving artist can attest. To support your creative Water energy, give yourself long periods of uninterrupted silence. Close the door, unplug the phone, or leave town. Do whatever it takes to free yourself from the constraints of the physical world in order to open to the mystical and divine.

Metal energy gets creative. Metal energy is intellectual, verbal, and analytical in nature. Metal gets creative by forming unique combinations of words, thoughts, or ideas. These combinations might be expressed in written form, through conversation over dinner, or as a computer program. However Metal chooses to express its creative force, it tends to use symbols and systems, rather than Earth energy's acts of kindness. Metal tends to look for a laboratory, a computer, or a classroom in which to create. If it cannot find one of these spaces, it will tidy up and create order in whatever space it finds itself. Organizing is Metal's way of bringing abstract systems and patterns into the physical realm.

A quiet and solitary place to sit and journal draws Water energy's creativity to the surface.

Wood energy gets creative. Wood energy thinks best on its feet. Fast and sure-footed, Wood does not understand why Water needs so much time to do everything. Decisions are made instantaneously and changed just as fast. Time is of the essence and productivity, not morality, is the highest value. Not to say that Wood energy is immoral. It simply finds no enjoyment in verification and paperwork, rather it delights in the discovery of something new.

Wood-energy people are the pioneers—those adventurous souls who dare to try something that has never been done before. To support your Wood, you simply need to get out of the way. Do not slow it down with long-range planning or conditions, let it grow unimpeded. If you are a Wood person, fill your creativity zone with the tools you need to embody your ideas in form, regardless of whether that form is a product, a paragraph, or a corporation. One caution, however. You love the creative stage, but hate to complete things. Find a way to pass your creations on to someone else who will bring them to completion or surround yourself with Metal energy that can help you finish what you start.

Fire energy gets creative. A sight, a sound, a taste, or a touch is all Fire needs to open into creative expression. Feeling stymied? Get a playmate or a pet. Creativity and play are one and the same for Fire energy and nothing will help you feel more creative than a person or pet who will play with you. Therefore, fill your creativity zone with all kinds of toys—a new motorcycle, a stunning CD collection, a blooming Christmas cactus—and invite others over to play.

With bright colors, fresh flowers, munchies, and all kinds of games, this room is set up to encourage playfulness in guests of all ages. Whether it is a midnight snack or an evening of movie watching, Fire enjoys inviting others over to play.

The renewal zone

Some individuals sleep best if they get to bed before 9:00 P.M.; others need to stay up until at least 11:00 P.M. in order to avoid a restless night. Your sleep style is an important consideration when setting up your renewal zone. If you tend to sleep in late, you will want blackout shades to keep the sunlight at bay. If you wake up before dawn, especially in the winter, you might want to add a sunrise alarm clock to slowly brighten the room. Even if you sleep a regular eight hours from 10:00 P.M. to 6:00 A.M., be certain to keep the following in mind:

Renewal is a Water-energy state. For this reason, standing under a hot shower can be as invigorating as six hours of sleep. If you have a difficult time getting to sleep, take a hot bath right before bedtime or deepen your sleep rhythm by adding the sound of running water in your room.

Avoid patterns. Renewal is a yin state. Solid colors are more yin in nature, whereas patterns are yang. Busy active patterns in your bedding can influence you even after the lights go out, since you hold the visual memory of the pattern in your head.

Use dark colors. Dark subdued colors, such as black and dark blue, generate Water energy and help people achieve a deeper more restful sleep. Try a week of midnight-blue sheets followed by a week of white sheets and see which ones help you sleep better.

New sunrise alarm clocks help you rise before dawn without aid of natural light. All have "simulated" dawn light. Some feature white noise to block out traffic and other unwanted sounds.

The neutral color scheme in this bedroom is restful and promotes healthful sleep. The red pillow, which adds a bit of passion, is easily thrown off the bed when it is time to sleep.

Acknowledgments

The visual element greatly enhances our understanding and integration of feng shui principles. Therefore, I am deeply appreciative of Marla Dee, Mark Grace, Cynthia Herning, Willamarie Huhlskamp, Nancy Matthews, Polly Reynolds, Paul & Stacey Richard, Julie Shipman, Ann Wilkinson, and the many other clients whose magnificent living spaces are depicted in this book. The very talented Kevin Dilley at Hazen Photography gave many days to this project, as did the talented crew at Chapelle, Ltd. Special thanks to Lana Hall for taking on such a challenging book, and to Jo Packham for believing in the power of feng shui to change lives for the better.

Resources

SELF START, Inc., 703 E. 1700 S., Salt Lake City, UT 84105. Provides advanced business training and mentoring for feng shui consultants, professional organizers, and life coaches. Contact Sharon through her web site at www.selfstart.net, call 801-519-9161, or e-mail her at fstc@xmission.com.

The Feng Shui Training Center. Provides core training for feng shui practitioners. Contact them at www.thefengshuitrainingcenter.com, call 801-519-9161, or e-mail Sharon at fstc@xmission.com.

Clear & Simple. Provides the only professional organizer certification training program in the United States. They also provide organizing support for homes and businesses throughout the US. Reach them at ClearSimple.com or call 801-463-9090.

Photo Credits

Michael Skarsten, Salt Lake City, UT: 32(t), 127
Jessie Walker, Glencoe, IL: 1, 3, 4(t)(b), 6, 8(b), 9, 10(r), 11, 12(t), 13(t)(b), 18, 19(b), 20(t)(b), 21(t), 22, 24, 27(b), 32(b), 35(r), 36, 42(tr), 46(b)(tr), 47, 50, 51, 52(t), 54–55, 60(t)(b), 61(t)(b), 62, 63,(t)(b), 66, 67, 68–69, 72–73, 74–75, 76, 78, 79, 80, 84, 85, 94(t), 97, 99, 102, 103, 105, 106(t), 107, 115(b), 116(bl), 117(br), 118(b), 119(tl), 122–123, 128(r), 130(b), 132(cl), 136, 137, 139(t)(l), 140, 145, 156, 157, 158(b)
Artville (©1997): 26
Corbis (©2000): 12, 58(tr)(b), 81, 82, 91(r), 134(tr)(b), 148(l), 151(b), 152(r), 153(t)
PhotoDisc (©1995, 1999, 2000, 2001): 22, 27, 30(tl)(bl), 35(l), 43, 49(bl)(br), 52(r), 57, 64(b), 83, 87, 91(l), 95, 109(tr), 111(r)(l), 117(cr), 122(ct)(br), 124, 129, 132(t)(c), 135(tl), 144, 148(tr)(br), 150, 151(t), 154, 155

About the author

Sharon's background in psychology led her to develop an approach to feng shui that reveals how one's deep psychological patterns surface in one's external environment. Having worked with hospitals and healers of numerous disciplines, Sharon integrates Chinese medicine, traditional feng shui teachings, Jungian psychology, and shadow-therapy work into her feng shui consultations.

She delights in helping clients discover their purpose and align their lives to support that purpose. Sharon currently runs Self Start, a training center in Salt Lake City, Utah, that provides advanced business training and mentoring for feng shui consultants, professional organizers, and life coaches. Sharon balances her work life with two amazing boys and a joyful marriage.

Index

Blockchain

for dummies®

A Wiley Brand

Blockchain

by Tiana Laurence

Blockchain For Dummies®

Published by: **John Wiley & Sons, Inc.**, 111 River Street, Hoboken, NJ 07030-5774, www.wiley.com

Copyright © 2017 by John Wiley & Sons, Inc., Hoboken, New Jersey

Published simultaneously in Canada

No part of this publication may be reproduced, stored in a retrieval system or transmitted in any form or by any means, electronic, mechanical, photocopying, recording, scanning or otherwise, except as permitted under Sections 107 or 108 of the 1976 United States Copyright Act, without the prior written permission of the Publisher. Requests to the Publisher for permission should be addressed to the Permissions Department, John Wiley & Sons, Inc., 111 River Street, Hoboken, NJ 07030, (201) 748-6011, fax (201) 748-6008, or online at http://www.wiley.com/go/permissions.

Trademarks: Wiley, For Dummies, the Dummies Man logo, Dummies.com, Making Everything Easier, and related trade dress are trademarks or registered trademarks of John Wiley & Sons, Inc. and may not be used without written permission. All other trademarks are the property of their respective owners. John Wiley & Sons, Inc. is not associated with any product or vendor mentioned in this book.

LIMIT OF LIABILITY/DISCLAIMER OF WARRANTY: THE PUBLISHER AND THE AUTHOR MAKE NO REPRESENTATIONS OR WARRANTIES WITH RESPECT TO THE ACCURACY OR COMPLETENESS OF THE CONTENTS OF THIS WORK AND SPECIFICALLY DISCLAIM ALL WARRANTIES, INCLUDING WITHOUT LIMITATION WARRANTIES OF FITNESS FOR A PARTICULAR PURPOSE. NO WARRANTY MAY BE CREATED OR EXTENDED BY SALES OR PROMOTIONAL MATERIALS. THE ADVICE AND STRATEGIES CONTAINED HEREIN MAY NOT BE SUITABLE FOR EVERY SITUATION. THIS WORK IS SOLD WITH THE UNDERSTANDING THAT THE PUBLISHER IS NOT ENGAGED IN RENDERING LEGAL, ACCOUNTING, OR OTHER PROFESSIONAL SERVICES. IF PROFESSIONAL ASSISTANCE IS REQUIRED, THE SERVICES OF A COMPETENT PROFESSIONAL PERSON SHOULD BE SOUGHT. NEITHER THE PUBLISHER NOR THE AUTHOR SHALL BE LIABLE FOR DAMAGES ARISING HEREFROM. THE FACT THAT AN ORGANIZATION OR WEBSITE IS REFERRED TO IN THIS WORK AS A CITATION AND/OR A POTENTIAL SOURCE OF FURTHER INFORMATION DOES NOT MEAN THAT THE AUTHOR OR THE PUBLISHER ENDORSES THE INFORMATION THE ORGANIZATION OR WEBSITE MAY PROVIDE OR RECOMMENDATIONS IT MAY MAKE. FURTHER, READERS SHOULD BE AWARE THAT INTERNET WEBSITES LISTED IN THIS WORK MAY HAVE CHANGED OR DISAPPEARED BETWEEN WHEN THIS WORK WAS WRITTEN AND WHEN IT IS READ.

For general information on our other products and services, please contact our Customer Care Department within the U.S. at 877-762-2974, outside the U.S. at 317-572-3993, or fax 317-572-4002. For technical support, please visit https://hub.wiley.com/community/support/dummies.

Wiley publishes in a variety of print and electronic formats and by print-on-demand. Some material included with standard print versions of this book may not be included in e-books or in print-on-demand. If this book refers to media such as a CD or DVD that is not included in the version you purchased, you may download this material at http://booksupport.wiley.com. For more information about Wiley products, visit www.wiley.com.

Library of Congress Control Number: 2017936813

ISBN 978-1-119-36559-4 (pbk); ISBN 978-1-119-36561-7 (ebk); ISBN 978-1-119-36560-0 (ebk)

Manufactured in the United States of America

10 9 8 7 6 5 4 3 2 1